Dear Mom

Thank You for

Love
Freddey

THE MAGIC OF
MENTORSHIP

LESSONS LEARNED FROM MY THREE DADS

**Life-changing messages that can
take your life to new levels of
success and happiness**

THE MAGIC OF MENTORSHIP

LESSONS LEARNED FROM MY THREE DADS

Life-changing messages that can
take your life to new levels of
success and happiness

FREDDY MCGAVER

A portion of the proceeds from book sales are donated to benefit youth wrestling though USA Wrestling.

Published by:
Bench Press Books
P.O. Box 180081
Delafield, WI 53018
www.theMagicofMentorship.com

Please contact the author or the publisher for quantity discounts for schools, non-profits, and other organizations.

ISBN: 978-1-59598-023-6

Library of Congress Number: 2011907497

Cover design by Kevin Gardner.
Interior design and typesetting by The Publishing Institute.

Printed in the United States of America.

This book is dedicated to all the HEROES
along my path who taught
me all kinds of life lessons,
and the many more
who continue to cross my path.

ACKNOWLEDGEMENTS

Having enjoyed the nurturing of a loving mother and father and the stability of a loving family, I am grateful for so many things it is impossible to mention them all here. But I'd like to try ...

As I reflect on my path, I can say that my many mentors and those I have had the honor of mentoring have motivated me to grow and continue to inspire me, to help me evolve to be the person I have become.

As a student at Marquette University, two of my teammates were Danny O'Neil and Chuck Karpfinger. Larry O'Neil and Barney Karpfinger, their dads, were the wrestling coaches at Marquette. In retrospect, I believe that many of the hundreds of athletes who participated in the wrestling program would say that these coaches became *their* dads, too. On behalf of all the young men who had the opportunity to compete under the leadership of those everyday heroes, I would like to thank the Karpfinger and O'Neil families for sharing their dads with us. Coach O'Neil and Coach Karpfinger taught us all life lessons that we remember each day. Larry O'Neil was also instrumental in my starting www.EncourageAmerica.org, which you'll learn more about in detail later in this book.

It's often said that you meet people for a reason, a season, or a lifetime. As I look back, there is only a handful of people with whom I've been able to share all three aspects of that saying. Let me explain. The reason I'm as strong as I am is that I wanted to improve at my sport. My obvious desire to get better drew me toward wanting to be part of the that team. I then got to know my other two "dads" for a season, and then another season, and then another. These powerful bonds and significant influences on me evolved into long-term friendships that now span more than three decades.

I am grateful for all of the experiences that have enriched me in so many ways. The openness and kindness of my three dads invited me to be open and kind myself.

My message to you throughout the following pages is: don't limit yourself. If you meet someone for a reason, for a season, or for a lifetime, you'll be enriched forever. You can't really get it wrong.

Other important influences in my life were my biological brothers—Charles, Joseph, and Richard—and sisters—Maryann and Christine.

From those early days of wrestling on, my passion for sports and continuous learning allowed me to meet more mentors and created an environment that helped me find even more mentors, who then became my adopted brothers and sisters. The following list includes many of those who have grown close to my heart and played important roles in my life. Thank you! I am grateful for your friendship.

Bob Allen
Jim Allen
Doug & Jeannie Andrewski
Jim Baker
Michael and Debbie Beining
Eileen Bodoh
Ray Bohl
Jos Boom
Rick Bower
Phil Buerk
Paul Burkhardt
Tom Burns
Phil Callen
A.J. Capelli
Sue Carlson
Paul Charnon
Chuck and Sue Coakley
Michael and Jo Coakley
Pete Davis
Mike Deschler
Linda Eckhardt
Jerry Emmerich &
    Christina Trompler
Michael End
David Feerick
Ron Fieber
Mike & Bernie Furlong
Frank and Cheryl Galka
Jerry Gates
Thomas Giebel
Constance Gilaspie
Scott Grudzinski
Ben Guido
Susan Harte
Vicki Hastings
Bob Healy
Russ and Nancy Hellickson
Harlow Hellstrom
Kira Henschel
Luke Hepp
Matt Hepp
Bill Hinkens
Pete Hirt
Mitch Hull
Dan Johnson

Dan and Mary Jones
Chuck Karpfinger
Jim Keepers,
Lee Kemp
Joe Kloiber
Tom Knitter
Kristin Kopp
Jim Koch
Bill Kumprey
James Langenkamp
Butch Lee
Greg Lehman
John Lehman
Sue Lehman
Reggie ("The Crusher") Lisowski
Tom Lutzow
Dale Maas
Dan Madigan III
Susie Mathews
Al McGuire
Paul McShane
Tom McShane
Joe McCook
Karen Meyer
Keith Michalak
Marty Mitchell
Kent Morin
Kevin Morin
Bill Morse
Bridget & Marty Mulgrew
Mark Mulqueen
Paul Mulqueen
Steve Nachreiner
Fred Nicklaus
Danny O'Neil
Michael O'Neil
Peter Ogden
Leon Pachowitz
Ulice Payne
Lenny Pepp
Ben Peterson
Jim Pogerlc
Scott Prosen
Tim Prosen
Bruce Purdy

Hank Raymonds
Andy & Susy Rein
Mark Richman
Sue & Kurt Roskopf,
Fritz Ruf
Rudy Ruiz
Sandy Ruffalo
Bob Rusch
Susan Russell
Katherine Scherer
James Schmitz
Jennifer and Joe Schubert
Dave Schultz
Mark Schultz
Nancy Schultz
Bob Seneff & his father,
    Robert G. Seneff
Joel Shilling
Laurent Soucie
Bob Steenlage
Bob Sweet
Toddy
Karen Tredwell
Tim Trovato
Gary Tsoumas
Saskia Van der Molen
Brian Weber
Kathy Weber
Nick Weber
Bob Weingard
Jack Weissgerber
Cal Wetzel
Ron Wied
Tom Wolf
Bill Young

FOREWORD

By Russ Hellickson

I was a collegiate wrestling coach for 36 years at two institutions. During the 16 years that I worked as an assistant or head coach at The University of Wisconsin and the twenty years I served as head coach at The Ohio State University, I worked with nearly 500 different athletes. Though most were collegiate student athletes, my own Olympic quests also allowed me to work and train with young men who shared a common drive for the highest level of international competition.

I found out very quickly in my career that I measured and evaluated all these athletes by the attitudes and efforts they displayed in training and in competition. It was crystal clear to me that a person's true personality and character surfaced when he was physically, mentally and psychologically tested on the wrestling mat. If you make a man drive himself to total fatigue and then force him to do more, any facade disappears. Throw a man one on one against the best around in front of those who know him well, and the real man emerges. Nothing phony and nothing artificial could ever survive this wrestling test. It was ironclad. In my world

Dan Gable (L.) with towel
and Russ Hellickson (R.) at
the US Wrestling Federation
nationals in North Carolina,
1975.

Russ Hellickson (R.) speaking with
Jeff Blatnick (L., 1984 Olympic
champion in Greco-style wrestling),
at the Olympic Games in Seoul,
South Korea, in 1988.

of wrestling, the BS was always stripped away. I wish I could assess and evaluate all people this easily.

If any of my athletes cared to know, I was more than willing to share my appraisal of them with them. I have hundreds of lifelong friends who shared this laboratory of wrestling with me. I know them. They know me. That's the way it ought to be.

Fred McGaver is one of those friends. He did well in my wrestling test.

I have known Freddy Mac for over thirty years. Though I did not have him as a student athlete in college, I witnessed his national exploits at Marquette University and was proud to have him on our Wisconsin Wrestling Club team that claimed National Freestyle team titles in the early 1980s.

Fred is a multi-faceted guy who also sold me one of my first life insurance policies. I was proud to help him in 1996, when he traveled from Milwaukee to Columbus, Ohio, to train for the Olympic wrestling trials. He surprised a lot of people when he finished near the top of the super heavy-weight division and American wrestling icon, Bruce Baumgartner. It was not a surprise to me.

I learned a lot about what and who had influenced and impacted Fred in his life through what he has shared in this book. His observations and real life experiences, recounted in his unique way have much to offer those willing to listen. I enthusiastically endorse the messages and the messenger.

My wrestling test measured Fred many times during his competitive days. Here are things that I know about Fred McGaver. He is a good friend. He is the most positive and optimistic person I have ever met. He does not discourage easily and he will encourage incessantly. He is reliable and accountable at all times and I trust him without reservation. He is one of the smartest people I know, but he will never tell you that. He respects the talents and abilities of others and will unselfishly and willingly work to make more of others by giving more of himself. But most of all, I know that he will never quit.

His life can change your life. His attitude can change your attitude. Read on.

—Russ Hellickson

Russ Hellickson graduated from the University of Wisconsin-Madison and worked on the family farm. He was later invited to become assistant wrestling coach for his alma mater under the leadership of Duane Kleven. He eventually became head coach, and in 1986 was hired by Ohio State University as their head wrestling coach through 2006. Russ was a silver medalist in the 1976 Olympics in Montreal, and was voted captain of the 1980 US Olympic Wrestling Team by his peers. The 1980 games were boycotted by the US teams because of the Soviet Union's invasion of Afghanistan. Russ was also a commentator for wrestling for the 1984, 1988, 1992, 1996, 2000, and 2004 Olympics. He is a member of the National Wrestling Hall of Fame.

I AM WRESTLING – DO NOT WEEP FOR ME

This speech was given as a farewell tribute to Marquette University wrestling at a gathering in Milwaukee, WI. on 11-3-01 by Ohio State Head Coach Russ Hellickson.

From the ancient walls of Samaria and from hieroglyphics written on the tombs of Egyptian kings, we know that wrestling is a sport of the ages.

It touches the lives of all who participate in it and many times even those who just observe it.

Who can forget the emotional victory of Jeff Blatnick over cancer before his Gold Medal win in Los Angeles in 1984 or the heart-rending upset victory of Rulon Gardner over previously undefeated wrestling icon Alexander Karelin in Australia at the 2000 Olympics.

You can see the impact of the sport in the eyes of even its youngest combatants. Perhaps in apprehension of that very first one-on-one or that glorious twinkling elation that comes from the first victory over the vanquished foe.

And for those who stay the course for a career, their eyes reflect a passion that penetrates deep into their very souls, a look that impacts for a lifetime and yes, a look that makes them what they are.

Here is an image I want to leave with each of you tonight:

I am Wrestling! Do not weep for me!!

Weep for those who will never experience me.

Weep for those who will never feel the exhausting pain of my training,

Weep for those who will never sense the bond of camaraderie that once established, will never wane or die.

Weep for those who will never comprehend the demands of my discipline

And most of all, weep for those poor souls who will never miss me, because they never knew me.

I am Wrestling! Do not weep for me!!

I have been experienced in virtually every culture and civilization known to mankind.

I have been contested in over 150 documented forms in written history.

There is no nation on this planet that throughout all time, has not experienced me.

I am Wrestling! Do not weep for me!!

Look to those seated around you and think of the qualities that make them what they are:

Accountability, responsibility, persistence, fortitude, strength, compassion, work ethic, ingenuity, determination, integrity, honesty, focus, diligence, and resolve.

Wrestling is not the only place they could acquire these, but by God ,they all reside here!! And if you live with me long enough these will become you.

I am Wrestling! Do not weep for me!!

No political agenda or political interpretation can ever destroy me. My merit and my worth is no threat to any cause, but rather through my values, I am a model for others.

I am Wrestling! Do not weep for me!!

Celebrate what I am, celebrate what I have been, celebrate what I represent, and celebrate the many ways I have impacted your life. I will survive this test as I have survived others. I am forever etched into the very fiber of all mankind.

The world needs me. Time is on my side.
History guarantees me!

I am Wrestling! Do Not weep for me!!

USA
wrestling

6155 Lehman Dr.

Colorado Springs, CO

80918

(719) 598-8181 ph.

(719) 598-9440 fx.

www.TheMat.com

PRESIDENT
James Ravannack

1st VICE PRESIDENT
Bruce Baumgartner

2nd VICE PRESIDENT
Greg Strobel

TREASURER
Van Stokes

SECRETARY
Rance Stein

EXECUTIVE DIRECTOR
Rich Bender

FILA
National Federation Member

U S A

Member, U.S. Olympic Committee

Dear Freddy,

Congratulations on the publication of your book titled "My Three Dads and The Life Changing Power of Mentorship."

I remember working with and learning from you in our college days though our pursuit of the World and Olympic Teams. It is amazing how our paths have intersected over our many years of training.

As I reflect on my days as the wrestling coach at Purdue University, I was reminded of how you helped my athletes train for the NCAA Division I Tournament when you were training to try out for the Olympic Team in your late 30s. It was interesting how you taught the younger men through your work ethic that they, too, could achieve more simply by hard work. This was no magic formula. You are a true example of what I believe, is that in order to succeed at something you must find a way to enjoy the journey. To compete so successfully as long as you did it takes a drive, a great work ethic and most importantly a way to enjoy the process. Everyone who has trained with you agrees that you have a strong work ethic and a real sense of fairness, both of which are ingrained in you. You were a training partner to many of the best wrestlers in the world for over 20 years, which is a testament to how your endurance and skill allowed you to succeed in and contribute to a very difficult sport. Everyone was well aware to not underestimate Freddy!

It was an honor for me to present you with the "Olympic Diploma" in 2001. The inscription read, "For a remarkable contribution, as a Volunteer, to the development of the sport of wrestling and Olympism, and to the promotion of friendship and solidarity among peoples." Your commitment to USA Wrestling as a competitor, coach and ambassador is proof of your loyalty to our sport and your willingness to help others. We are also very appreciative of your generosity in contributing part of the proceeds from your book to support USA Wrestling National Teams. Your support will help benefit some of the over 150,000 athletes who participate in our programs, which feed into the teams that represent the US in various World and Olympic wrestling competitions.

Best wishes for continued success as you take a stand for what is good in our society by inviting and encouraging so many to engage in mentorship.

It is said the work of a teacher or coach will last for generations.

Thanks again for making a difference.

Sincerely

Mitch Hull
Director of National Teams
2X USA World Team

MESSAGE FROM THE CO-AUTHOR

I met Freddy in June of 2009. I was performing background music for a reception at the Entrepreneur's Conference in Milwaukee when he came up to me, sat down and started chatting about *Encourage America*. I wasn't sure what to make of Freddy at first, but listened to what he was saying and found I was interested. There was just something about his presence that made me want to talk with him, so I sought him out at the meeting the next day. We ended up chatting and, as I learned more about *Encourage America* and the intensity of his desire to share his story with others, we starting chatting about this book.

Freddy had been writing down stories for at least a couple of years and was trying to figure out how to turn the rough manuscript into a book that would be interesting to a range of audiences. I think the audience he is most interested in teaching is teenagers, followed closely by their families, friends, teachers, employers, and anyone else who is interested in approaching life from a more positive perspective.

Freddy's message is personal and universal at the same time. He speaks directly from his heart in a manner that most people I know would find uncomfortable because it requires allowing oneself to be emotionally exposed and vulnerable.

Freddy and I started working together on his manuscript shortly after we met in 2009. It's been a process of fits and starts, depending on how each of us was feeling at the time. It's also been incredibly fun. We decided that the most efficient way to get Freddy's stories down on paper was to have him talk and have me type. I would edit as I typed and ask questions as we went along to make sure the story was clear. One running joke was that I was responsible for making sure that the words "so" and "but" never start a sentence.

The stories are powerful and the lessons are both big and small. Sometimes the small lessons teach the biggest lessons. Freddy talks about his family as an important, yet flawed, influence, as are all families. He speaks about wrestling as a great passion, source of satisfaction, and place to focus his incredible energy and intensity. He speaks about business as a test of personal strength and ethics. He also talks about working hard, yet not quite making it to the pinnacle, even though he excelled more than 99.9% of the people who take up a sport or profession. It is a bittersweet lesson to work that hard and make it that far, but not make the summit, as they say in mountaineering.

On the other hand, it is a testament to his determination, strength, intelligence, and work ethic that Freddy has succeeded at the level he has in his life. It's all a matter of perspective: disappointment or gratitude. Each of us has the opportunity to choose which perspective to take. I choose to take the perspective of gratitude. I've found that every experience contains a lesson, that if I learn it, will improve my life. If I choose to ignore the lesson, it will just be presented again and again until I pay attention. When I approach experiences with an attitude of gratitude, I learn my lessons more quickly and my life is better.

I hope that each person who reads this book will come to the same realization. No one else can do the work for you—it has to be your choice to look for the positive and be open to the things you need to learn. It's all around us—we just need to be aware.

—Susan Carlson
Accede CPA

Sue Carlson was raised in northern Wisconsin and traveled to Tampa, Florida, to attend the University of Tampa to study Management Information Systems on an Air Force ROTC scholarship. Following graduation, she joined the Wisconsin Air National Guard in Madison, WI, and pursued her MBA. She has since worked as an administrator of basic and biomedical research programs at the University of Wisconsin–Madison; served as director of Operations for WiCell Research Institute; authored, edited and managed the development of high school textbooks for on-line delivery; and is now co-owner of Accede CPA, a Madison-based company devoted to helping small businesses and non-profits by providing back-office services. In the process of doing all these things, she developed an acute awareness of the need to be aware of the lessons being presented and the importance of making the effort to learn them the first (or second) time around. This one piece of knowledge has improved her life tremendously.

PREFACE

This book is about the many experiences that have had a profound effect on my life. You will find it is not a continuous story and does not flow like other books you may have read. It is a compilation of stories about my experiences that also contain powerful life lessons.

In this collection, I intend to share the joy of some of my wins and the consequences of many of the losses in my life. My goal is to be open about my life and simply make the point that I have let go of my need to be a tough guy by wrestling or a rich guy through my business ventures. I have met Olympic and World champions from many sports and have learned that we all have a sport or an area in our life in which we are grossly inadequate to compete. It was lucky for these champions that they found where they fit as their stars lined up to elevate them to Olympic glory. The true champions in my life are those who have discovered balance.

The *Encourage America* story, which appears later in the book, is a detailed sharing of a low point along my life's path. I was challenged to do something about which I was so boldly complaining: negative news.

Have you heard of the proverb, "Never complain about something you tolerate?" I decided to work on this project and it has become a way of life for me. Each day, I share with people I meet how everyone can make a difference in their lives by acknowledging the positive aspects of their lives. We all get what we give. Join in and give good stuff.

Please do not confuse the fact that I've learned these lessons with the idea that I have already arrived, that I know it all, or that I have it and you don't. It is my belief that we are each on a path, our personal path, to live out our souls' purposes.

Your soul purpose is as individual as the fingerprints on your hands. If every fingerprint on every hand is perfect and we can each accept that our individual paths are perfect for what we each need to accomplish on the soul level, then we will be better equipped to let go of judgments about various experiences. The judgments I typically experience are: I failed, I didn't measure up, I did this or that wrong, or any of the hundreds of other negative comments that we each tell ourselves throughout the each day.

I learned at a young age that our words are very powerful. It is with the power of words in mind that I have become more diligent in my own self-talk.

I invite you to learn from my lessons, which were sometimes very painful and sometimes fun, so that you may improve your self-talk and enhance the travels along your path. Since there is only one source of "knowledge," I thank those who taught me these lessons and acknowledge that every lesson I learned was taught to me by someone else. I thank the mentors, teachers, and friends who showed me the sides of myself I needed to see and that I might have never discovered without their guidance.

Usually, when books are written, authors title the book at the end of the process. In this situation, I created the title first and then immediately remembered how we are always learning from each other.

To the families of Larry O'Neil and Barney Karpfinger, I am one of the thousands of people they influenced over the years in coaching and in business. My story is similar to the stories of the many other kids they coached in that they made a profound impact on our lives. Knowing that love is abundant, I am aware that these two dads, whom I adopted, have created hundreds of relationships with young athletes, who also agree that Barney and Larry were dads to them in many ways. I thank the families of Barney and Larry for sharing your dads with all of us.

It is said that the work of a teacher can last for generations. Although Larry and Barney coached wrestling, they taught us about life as they trained us to wrestle.

The following speech by President Theodore Roosevelt, entitled *Citizenship in a Republic* at the Sorbonne, Paris, France, on April 23, 1910, has always been an inspiration to me, and it reminds me of all three of my dads:

> *It is not the critic who counts, nor the man who points out how the strong man stumbles or where the doer of deeds could have done better. The credit belongs to the man who is actually in the arena, whose face is marred by dust and sweat and blood, who strives valiantly, who*

errs and comes up short again and again, because there is no effort without error or shortcoming, but who knows the great enthusiasms, the great devotions, who spends himself for a worthy cause; who, at the best, knows, in the end, the triumph of high achievement, and who, at the worst, if he fails, at least he fails while daring greatly, so that his place shall never be with those cold and timid souls who knew neither victory nor defeat.

PART 1

THE BOY FROM CUDAHY, WISCONSIN

Young Freddy, age 9

Family photo from 1960. My parents' 15th wedding anniversary. From left to right:
Christine, MaryAnn, Charles, Mom, Dad, Joseph, Freddy, and Richard.

Charles and Joseph McGaver, ages 3 and 1 (1949).

FAMILY AND FAMILIAR

I am the youngest of six children and I learned that we all have at least two families: the family we come from and the family we create. The family we come from is typically composed of blood relatives. The family we create has more multidimensional connections.

Although I have three biological brothers and two biological sisters, the things we have in common are from the earlier parts of our lives. Everyone has grown in different directions from the time we used to sleep under one roof. As years go by, you wake up and realize you're living different lives. Being thankful for the family I came from has helped me to be more aware of the family I've created. This family consists of mentors, teammates, coworkers, and the dearest of friends, all of whom have helped me to become more of what I need to be. When you read the definition of the word family, you will see that it says "family is that which is familiar."

I once wrote a poem and I remember a couple of verses that apply here:

It is mainly our differences that motivate us
to find similarities that we all seem to share.
It is also our need to be needed and want to be
wanted that makes us want to care.
As I need your smiles, and you seem to want
mine, there is no better time
To express my gratitude for you in my life
than at this very time.

By being open about your life and willing to learn from and about others, the familiar aspects of other people's lives will enlarge your family as you develop close relationships with the people who become important in your life.

THE EARLY YEARS

I grew up in a small town called Cudahy, Wisconsin. Cudahy is located on Lake Michigan, east of the Milwaukee Metropolitan Airport and about 90 miles north of Chicago, and has a population of 18,000 people. It is

a typical blue-collar town with plenty of parks and a beautiful lake to enjoy. Cudahy was a wonderful place to grow up. Over the years, I've heard first hand from many people the judgments they have on my home-town. I always had to smile as I asked them if they had ever been to Cudahy and they would usually say no. I still tell people when this topic comes up that they have no idea what they are talking about when they rip on a small town like Cudahy.

I agree that every community has its challenges, but small town America is where I am from and I have a great respect for the values that are shared and learned by growing up in that environment. It is obvious that many small towns have an energy of their own and often provide the best environment for raising a family. With Lake Michigan as our east boundary and being just six miles south of downtown Milwaukee, it is a great place to live.

The McGaver residence, 1948 to 1977, Cudahy, WI

I attended private schools from second grade through my college years. My grade school years were at St. Frederick's, with high school years at Pio Nono (Latin for "Pius IX") for two years, St. Thomas More for two years, and then five years at Marquette University.

My parents were both employed outside the home. My father was a machinist. My mother was a registered nurse (Marquette University School of Nursing, 1942). We always had what we needed, and, as I remember, most of what we wanted.

Eleonore McGaver, Graduation, 1942

My two oldest brothers, Charlie and Joe, contracted polio when they were toddlers and had difficulty walking. My parents tended to be very protective of their oldest children, and did not allow them to play contact sports growing up. This did not diminish their sense of competition or will to excel, but I was the only athlete in the family, which drew me to find other mentors.

It was instilled in me at a very young age that I would have the opportunity to go to college and the focus was on getting my schooling.

I completed high school at Thomas More High School because the school I started at (Pio Nono High School) merged with another all boys private high school (Don Bosco High School) to create a new school called St. Thomas More High School. At that age, the world is small and it is unlikely

St. Thomas More High School, Milwaukee, Wisconsin

My parents' 25th wedding anniversary. From left to right: Freddy, Richard, Charles, Mom, Dad, Joseph, Christine, and Maryann.

that many teenagers can grasp how small it all is because of the strong influences our peers can have on us.

This peer pressure plays an important role in how we are able to adjust to being a part of a team or group as we join these groups to learn a sport or a skill and develop stronger friendships. My high school experience was a great value to me in many ways. I've told many of my friends who have kids, when they ask about private schools, that when teenagers get to a certain point, it seems many parents lose them as they start to grow up and establish their identities. I found that the peer pressure from my high school years was very powerful in a positive way.

When I graduated from high school, 98 percent of our 240 graduates went on to some higher learning institution. It was not an issue of if I was going to college, but where I was going to college. When your peers are focused on excelling in various areas of their lives and you want to hang out with them, it is easy to see how this peer influence can be very helpful in many ways.

In my early twenties, I finished college at Marquette University with a degree in business, which included a very well diversified curriculum of economics, management, and marketing classes, along with several journalism classes.

Upon graduation, I interviewed with many companies, two of them being the beer companies in Milwaukee: Pabst and Miller. I had the opportunity to work with both. In those days, the position I applied for was working on a route to visit beer customers, typically bars and restaurants, and getting them to purchase more of the product. As I recall, the position paid about $24,000 a year, and included a car and an expense account of about $100/week, which I would have used to buy drinks or other treats as they went around from bar to bar to get their orders.

I had another offer from a roofing company to work in sales and a few other offers to work in industrial products, working as a telemarketer, a stepping stone position to eventually become a sales rep. I ended up going into the insurance business on a commission-only basis. I guess because of my background in wrestling, I've always been drawn to high-risk situations and thrived on the opportunity to be accountable.

WHEN MY FATHER MET MY MOTHER (DAD'S VERSION)

Dad worked as a welder at the Ladish Company in Cudahy. The company was instrumental in making equipment used in World War II and beyond. The plant occupies a significant area of the six square miles covered by the town of Cudahy.

One day, my father burned his arm, so he went to the nurse, who happened to be my mother. When you have a burn, you have to go back every day to have your bandages changed. He would wait in line and sometimes let others go ahead of him, just so he could go to that nurse. About the third day, she asked why he always got her, and he said it must be another lucky day and smiled.

For several weeks, he went back to the nurse's office, even after his burn was healed, and she would say, "There's nothing wrong with you," and bark at him to go back to work. He would ask if she wanted to go out for coffee. After a few months of his politely persistent visits, she agreed to meet him. Shortly after that, he got to meet her parents.

Dad grew up in a small town called Fairchild, Wisconsin, 250 miles away from where he lived in Cudahy. He had a few sisters who lived nearby with their own families. He told me the story that when he met my mom's parents, he was amazed at what nice people they were. To him, her father was the kind of guy he wanted to become.

When my dad spoke of his own father, it was always with sadness and disappointment because his father used to drink hard and was often unkind to his mother. Coupled with the fact that he was the youngest of his family of 13 kids, and his father was 48 when he was born and his mother was 44, my dad was obviously not a planned child. My father would remind me in little ways, all the years I was growing up, that his dad never really bonded with him. My dad was 17 when he left the house he grew up in and moved to Cudahy. He was able to work in a business that his sister and her husband owned for a couple of years.

Mom's father, Stanley Wojcik, could fix or repair anything. He taught my dad a lot of skills. In 1951, just six years after my parents married, Mom's father died of cancer.

My parents' wedding, June, 1945

Both my parents were really sad for a long time. My dad's own mother passed away the same year, which was very hard on him because he was very close to his mother.

He told me, "I cannot imagine what my life would have been like if I hadn't met your mother, or if her parents had not been as kind to me as they were. I understand that the dynamics of families change all the time and that wherever you are is where you are. That's okay." It just took him eighty some years to say that sentence. As my father told these stories, it was obvious that he deeply loved and respected my mother's parents.

Dad was very deliberate about many things in his life, such as the things you do and don't do. One of the things to do was to be kind. He always said "Thank you," which you'll hear more about later in this book.

COMPARING YOURSELF
TO OTHERS

There's an old proverb that says, "To want to be another person is to waste the person you are." When people think about it, they don't really want to be anyone else. They just want that aspect of life that the other person has, whether it is money, fame, attractiveness, having social prestige, or whatever. However, all of these things come from learning to love ourselves.

This is a lesson I'm still learning today. It's impossible to compare your fingerprint to someone else's and expect them to match. Knowing that it's impossible, why compare anything else? I understand that in schools, there are test standards, requirements and expectations, but don't get sucked in to comparing yourself to others because when you compare, you always lose. Even if you compare yourself with someone who may have less than you, who may be less fit than you, who may have less schooling than you, I'm sure if you reflect just a few more minutes, there will also be areas where you don't come up to snuff against the other person's strengths. Comparing yourself to others is always a dead end.

I learned long ago that it doesn't matter what others think—it matters what you think. The opinions of others are their opinions, and should be left as their opinions and not become your beliefs. I never got caught up in accepting the opinions of others as my beliefs. Often, the opinions of others are expressions of their own limitations. Believing the opinions of others can be a problem for you only if you embrace them as being true.

PICKED ME UP
LIKE A BABY

One day, in 2003, I was asked to come over to my parents' house and help my father get dressed. He had recently had a stroke. After he had his first stroke, it was difficult for him to walk, or even stand without the aid of a wall, walker or person.

On that particular day, I was helping him in the bathroom and he was standing right next to the bathtub. Imagine me on one knee holding onto a strap around his waist with one hand, helping him keep his balance, and with the other hand, pulling up his pants after he had used the bathroom. He started to lean in slow motion toward the bathtub and was about to fall. I stepped into the bathtub and picked my father up with his upper body draped over my shoulder and his hips against my chest. The ordeal only lasted a few short seconds, and I was able to stabilize him, then walk him out of the bathroom and lay him down on his bed. Neither one of us said a word.

Once he was sitting safely back on his bed, I said to him in a nurturing, playful way, "Hey, Daddy Mack, where were you going on me, where were you going?"

He said, "I was going to fall in the bathtub, but somehow you scooped me up like a baby."

At that, I thought and said, "Well, you're okay now. We just have to make sure nothing like this happens again. If you notice you're going to fall, it is important that you tell me right away."

I finished getting him dressed and walked him over to the living room and sat him down in his favorite chair. A few minutes later, I was using the phone and my mother set him up with a TV tray because she'd prepared breakfast for him.

He then said, "Eleonore, I want to tell you something, but it is important that you let me finish."

She said, "What is it?"

"A few minutes ago, I was in the bathroom and Freddy was helping me get dressed when I started to fall into the bathtub. As I was falling, Freddy stepped into the bathtub and picked me up like a baby. Eleonore, it was amazing. I thought I was going to fall, but he picked me up, carried me back into the bedroom, and set me down on the bed. He picked me up like I was a baby. I think my baby son is the strongest man ever met. I weigh 240 pounds and he picked me up."

I was on hold the whole time he was talking to my mother. It was nice to hear my father say that. In those few moments, I also noticed how much I really wanted his approval.

A few minutes later, my mother motioned for me to come back into the bedroom so my father couldn't hear our conversation. In a hushed voice, he asked, "Did Dad fall?"

"Almost, but I was able to scoop him up before he did."

She then said, "Be careful. Just be careful." My mother talked to everybody that way when it concerned the care of my father. She demonstrated her amazing love always.

Eventually, my father was placed in a nursing home. My eldest brother would come every evening to get my father ready for bed. It was something to see. They had a system, brushing his teeth, sitting on the toilet, washing his hands and face, physically picking him up and putting him on the bed, positioning him on his side, and inserting pillows as he requested so he would be comfortable for the night. For three years, my brother was there every night. Maybe he missed just a couple times when he had to be with his wife or kids at some event. The rest of us took turns getting Dad ready for the day. We all understood, "Be careful. Just be careful."

It was very special to be able to observe the loyalty of my eldest brother and the love my father received as he was cared for each day and night by his family. When Dad was placed in a nursing home, every day, one or more of us kids would make it a priority to visit. I would often come to visit them even for fifteen minutes, only to find that one of my siblings was there before me or coming in when I left.

With the LOVE of my mother and the leadership of my eldest brothers, we pulled together.

FEAR OF DYING

About six months before my father passed away, my mother was telling me that he was going through a hard time and was afraid to die.

I said, "Maybe I should talk to him."

Of course, because I'm the baby of the family, I've often been treated and regarded like I'm still the baby, without the life experience or understanding that gives me insight into these things or the ability to share these thoughts with others. I suspect it's partially because I'm the youngest and partially because I never had my own family like my siblings did. People often thought that I didn't know about kids, having kids, having the responsibilities of a spouse, and being on the path of the happy family life and everything else that goes with it.

I recall telling my father that I never really met a woman who got my total attention in every way, so I could spoil her like he took care of my mom. It was interesting, because looking at their marriage, at least the part I got to see, my father really was a good provider in many ways, although my mother worked full time, because they, as parents, had different goals than other parents, like private education, which generated more expenses.

In the last couple of years of my father's life, it was clear that my mother was taking care of my father all the time. He was in a nursing home across a breezeway from the assisted living home where my mother lived until she required more care and moved to the same nursing home where my dad once resided. She would often walk over to spend the day with my father. Their day would often be broken up by visits from all six of us kids.

Just about every day, every one of us children showed up. The nurses would comment to my mother how amazing it was that they got to know our family so well because one of us would usually be there. I would often see my siblings on the way in or out, as we would be going about our lives.

*   *   *

Back to the story. Mom said in her protective, motherly voice, "What are you going to say to him?"

I said, "I don't know. I'll listen and see what I notice and what I think. Well, you can be there and hear what I say." I agreed to stop by the next day. I got there at 9:00 a.m. and I left five hours later.

During that time, my mother came and went several times because she was taking care of some of her daily chores. Coming in and out of the picture, she would conveniently show up when our conversation was less charged and more neutral. There was one period, for an hour and a half, when my father shared what it was like when he met my mother and he got to learn about her family.

Dad shared some things that he was really sad about that happened in his life, too. I told him that not even God can change the past. Even though we don't have to accept things as necessarily good things in our lives, some level of acceptance can often free us from being held hostage by them. Even though those things that made him really sad happened, he could be thankful for the outcome, because in retrospect, things worked out well for everyone.

During our conversation, I mentioned to Dad that Mom said he was afraid to die. I asked what was going on.

He said, "Sure, I'm afraid to die."

I said, "Well, what's going on?"

"I'd like to see what's going on with their lives. If I'm not here, I'm going to miss out," he told me.

I said, "Are you sure you're going to miss out? What do you mean? What if you could get to the other side and you would find out that what you really thought you'd miss out on, you'd get to see from another dimension. What if you could still talk to the kids in your dreams, like your mother has probably talked to you, (he said his mom had come to him in his dreams before) and give them the tidbits and insights they need so they can be protected to have a better life? What would that be like?"

He said, "If I knew that was true, then I'd be ready to go, because I guess I could be more helpful watching the whole group than watching them one at a time."

I began to share with him a meditation I once ran across, where you say a sentence and then you notice whatever you notice. The meditation goes like this: "Let it happen that everyone has peace."

We continued with this meditation process, which involved merely repeating the sentence over and over again, probably 200 times or more. It was obvious that he experienced a shift from a fear of dying to acceptance of his path.

*   *   *

Maybe you, like I have been many times, are afraid of the path you are on, only to find out that acceptance is an easier way than resistance.

If you find that you feel resentment or sadness about someone or some event in your life, you just might want to play with this meditation. I often find myself doing it when I am experiencing any kind of discomfort with any type of relationship. I will say, "Let it happen that [person's name] have peace." I focus on those words and say the phrase out loud many times [50 to 100 times] and then I ask, "Let it happen that everyone gets what they need." I am always amazed how miracles still exist in my everyday life as I practice this simple meditation.

MRS. BARRER

A woman in her seventies named Mrs. Barrer lived two blocks from my house from the time I was eleven to sixteen. Mrs. Barrer had grown up in Illinois and came to Cudahy as a young woman with her husband, where they raised their family of four children, who moved to different parts of the country after they grew up. Mrs. Barrer continued to live in the house her husband built for her in 1924. I had the opportunity to be her lawn boy, rake her leaves, and shovel her snow.

She was a very generous woman in terms of keeping me accountable. For example, on Wednesday nights, after 6:30 but before 7:30, I was supposed to go by the house to help

Mrs. Barrer's house

her take out the garbage. This typically involved walking about one hundred feet with two to three bags of garbage, so it was not a lot of work. It was obvious to me in later years, when I drove by her house and thought about those days, that she really had not needed me to take the garbage out because she would walk to the post office six blocks away just to go for a walk.

One day, I arrived at 7:45. She said, "Too late, Freddy, I just took it out at 7:30. You'll have to learn to be on time." This is a lesson I'm still learning because I don't always plan my time properly.

One day, I was half way through cutting Mrs. Barrer's grass and she called me into the house by standing on the porch waving her hand. I turned off the mower and she said I had to come in right away. There was a glass of ice water next to her chair and she said I had to come in and watch the moon landing. We were riveted to the TV set. That was forty years ago.

As we sat there, she told me, "My father fought in the Civil War. When I got married, we went about eight miles from the church we were married in to my husband's parents' house for the reception with the closest of family to celebrate our wedding. It took us over two hours to get that short distance in a horse and buggy. Now we're watching a man walk on the moon. I can't imagine what your life will be like when you get to be my age."

Forty years ago, there were no fax machines, no cell phones, no e-mail, no PDAs. Fast forward forty years from now. Considering how information doubles every time at twice the speed it did the previous time, it will be absolutely amazing to see what our world is like in four decades.

Mrs. Barrer also taught me how to knit. When I was fourteen years old, I broke my foot because of some horseplay and I had a cast on while it healed. She taught me how to knit a bootie for my cast. I was so excited about my bootie that I was telling some of the kids at school and got teased for being a little "Susie Homemaker."

Mrs. Barrer taught me how to make homemade caramels, as well. When Christmas rolled around, she would make and sell over 2,000 pounds of hand-dipped chocolates created in a special kitchen in her home. There would be nuts, nougat, coconut, and many other types of chocolates. Throughout the year, she offered to have me drop off boxes of chocolates that had been sold to people within a few block radius. She would always tell me to say, "Mrs. Barrer appreciates your business." This remains one of the adages I've used throughout my own entrepreneurial ventures.

She would often give me little bags of candy samples and say, "This is for your parents and this is for you. I want them to call me to tell me how much they enjoyed them, so I know they got them." She'd always give me a big bag to make sure they got some, if not all, of them. She always said, "Sweet tooth can lead to no tooth. Be careful of the sweet tooth."

The last time I saw Mrs. Barrer, I was sixteen years old and coming home from ice skating about 9 p.m. on a Friday night. I saw police cars and ambulance lights at her house. I ran up to the house and asked one of the police officers what had happened. He said, "We got a call to pick someone up. I'm assisting on the call." About a minute later, a stretcher holding Mrs. Barrer was carried down the stairs by some burly firemen.

Running up to her side, I said, "Mrs. Barrer, Mrs. Barrer, what's going on? Are you okay?"

In her alert voice, "I'm having a little trouble, but I'll be okay and you'll do fine, too."

She passed away from heart issues that very night. Mrs. Barrer was one of the first people I was close to who died.

Mrs. Barrer was a woman of strong faith, with a tremendous sense of community. I'm sure there are many more lessons I learned from Mrs. Barrer than the few I mention here.

THIRTY-TWO YEARS
AND FIVE MINUTES

The year was 1968. As you may recall, my father was forty years older than I was. He was the youngest in his family, the eldest being twenty years older. In between the oldest and youngest of thirteen kids, he had a lot of sisters. One of his sisters happened to be twelve years older than my dad. Auntie Faye, as I called her, was like a surrogate grandmother to me.

One time, Auntie Faye invited her grandson (my cousin), Eddie Senger, and me to go to the State Fair. I was twelve and he was eight.

* * *

As a side note, I just always remember numbers. It's funny how I'll remember someone's birthday rather than his or her name. People ask how I get to know birthdays. I work in the insurance industry. I ask names, birthdays, income, etc., and if it's important enough to ask, it's important enough to remember.

* * * *

That day, a hot muggy day at the beginning of August, we took the bus from Cudahy to State Fair Park, about five miles north and five miles west of where I lived. Auntie Faye had packed a lunch for us, which included non-pop-top cans of soda and peanut butter and jelly sandwiches.

Both my parents were working that day, so couldn't come to the fair. Auntie Faye, Eddie, and I walked around to look at the animals. We ended up in a general picnic area that was close to different booths, one of which had a man who drew caricatures. Being the inquisitive twelve year old I was, I asked my aunt if I could walk over there and watch what the guy was doing. After a few minutes, she waved me back, so I went back and ate my sandwich. I asked if I could go back because I wanted to ask him some questions. She said that we should eat our meal together, and then we could go over together. She said, "You might need to ask permission to talk to him, because he might need to concentrate on what he's doing."

The artist's booth was set up so that the person he was drawing sat in the chair, with the poster paper he used to make his sketches in front of him. There were several chairs against the wall in the booth. Each time someone's picture was finished, people would move to the next chair as they moved one closer to being his next subject.

I asked him if he minded if I asked questions and he said sure. I asked how long it took to draw a picture and he responded usually around five minutes. He charged about $2 for each caricature. To put this in perspective, in 1968, the minimum wage in America was $0.85 per hour. Doctors made about $100 a day and they were doing really great. He was charging $2 for a caricature. I mentioned that if he could draw ten caricatures an hour at $2 each, he could make $20 an hour. He smiled and said, "You're pretty good at math."

He kept drawing and seemed very content doing his art, knowing that he was creating a lasting memory that people would keep for many years. He took pride in including all kinds of details. Even their clothing or certain unique features would show up in his sketches. My aunt, my cousin, and I must have watched him for half an hour.

"The way you draw those pictures seems pretty easy," I said.

He replied, "Well, even though it only takes me about five minutes to do one of these drawings, it's taken me thirty-two years to get my time down to five minutes and keep the quality and detail at the best possible level."

I never forgot "...thirty-two years and five minutes."

"ORIENTATED"

I n 1975, I took a speech class at Marquette University with Professor Joseph Staudacher. Each week, we had to give speeches for three to five minutes about various topics of our choosing that would be informative, extemporaneous, persuasive, argumentative, and so on.

One week, I was giving a speech and I used the word "orientated." We all learn from our environment and experiences and some people in my life would say "orientated." After I was done speaking, I thought I had done a good job. Professor Staudacher said, "I'm going to give you a D because when you said the word 'orientated,' you lost me. The word 'orientated' must be your word because it is not a word in the English language. The word, properly pronounced, is 'oriented.'"

In front of over thirty other classmates, I got to learn how to spell the word "oriented." I must admit that afterwards, I never used the word "orientated" again and was able to figure out that I could probably change other beliefs in my life just as fast once I made the decision.

FEELINGS

We've all had feelings of fear, sadness, loneliness, inadequacy, self-doubt, anger, hopelessness, or helplessness, and sometimes we can talk ourselves into believing that we really are our feelings.

Have you watched water flow through a clear, plastic hose? If you imagine for a second that you are the hose and the feelings are the water, you will find that you are never any of those feelings. If you can be attentive to the label and the judgments you are having or may have had, you can let all those feelings flow through you and not get stuck.

Whenever you're feeling anything, remember that a feeling is a feeling—it's not you. You are not the anger. You are not the self-doubt. Unless you won't let the feeling flow. Then you own it. When that happens, the feeling really owns you.

TEARS—
THE MARK OF A MAN

Although I'm not close to my biological brothers now, as we were growing up, we were pretty connected.

My brother Joe had a friend named Butch, who was a Marine. One day, Joe got a phone call (we had the kind of phone that hung on the wall). The family often jokes that because I'm only 5'9" and my brothers are 6'1", 6'2" and 6'3", I am the runt of the litter. Suffice it to say that my brother is also a big guy.

He was not on the phone long and I remember being with my father in the kitchen, where the phone hung on the wall, as we observed the phone call. When Joe hung up the phone, he hung it up so hard it ripped the phone off the wall. He said, "Butch was killed in Vietnam."

As tears rolled down his face, he began to walk out the door and my dad stood up to cut him off at the pass and ask where he was going because he could see how serious Joe's mood was. Joe said he was going to Butch's mom's house. Butch wasn't his birth name. His name was Donald. Butch's father, Charles, had passed away just the year before. Now Butch's mom lost her husband one year and her son the next. Those are tremendous losses for anyone to endure.

My father said, "I'd have you call us when you get there, but the phone doesn't work." My brother apologized and my dad said, "Just make sure you don't drive fast. In fact, drive a little slower than you usually drive." Joe promised that he would and he returned in a couple of hours. He was talking to my parents and I wanted to hang out and find out what was going on. Mom asked me to come back later because she and my dad really needed to talk privately with Joe.

In 1968, I was twelve years old. When I was eleven, Butch had come by the house with Joe to show me his new car. He was taking my brother for a ride; I wanted to go along and Butch let me do so, and I got to sit in between them. Then Butch slid me up onto his lap and said, "As long as we're going, you might as well steer," and he let me steer.

After about a block, it was obvious I wasn't doing too well and I got back in the middle, but it was pretty cool to be eleven years old and steering a car. What I remember most about Butch was that he had a younger brother, a little younger than I was, and that he was always kind to me. I remember my father commenting that Butch was always very respectful.

About two weeks passed after Butch's death, the day of the funeral arrived. I was raised in the Catholic church, which has a tradition of young boys becoming altar boys. I was one of the two altar boys for the funeral. I remember Butch's mom. I never saw such sadness in all the years I've lived. When she cried, it was a shrill howl that went straight to my core and showed the intensity and significance of her loss. I will never forgot that. I know that event affected my brother Joe, but to this day, I've never heard how he ever dealt with his loss.

Fast forward to 1991. Butch had a brother named Joseph, a year younger than Butch, whom they used to call "Bobo."

My brother Rick is a fireman in Cudahy. Of all the siblings, he's the only one who has been a lifelong resident of the city. One day, Rick was on duty and he got a call that someone had been found down on the lakeshore at the bottom of a sixty-foot bluff. He and another firefighter worked together to bring the guy up to the top of the hill. When he got to the top of the hill, he recognized Bobo. They tried to revive him, but were unsuccessful. The tragic news traveled and soon I was at another funeral.

The funeral was held in the same church, but twenty-some years later. As the service progressed, I remembered glimpses of what I experienced when I was twelve. When we went to the cemetery, I happened to be with Mark Mulqueen, one of my wrestling mentors.

After prayers were said, there was an opportunity for everyone to pass by and pay their last respects in front of the casket. As the people were doing this, the closest of family always observes because the family expresses their wishes last, of all the people, so they can have some time for themselves.

As I received the baton with holy water from Mark Mulqueen, I expressed my intentions in front of the casket and then turned, passing it to the next person. As I turned, Bobo's mom recognized me and she said, "Freddy," then started to stumble a bit and lost her footing, and started to cry with the same howl, and she said, "Oh, Freddy..."

I scooped her up to keep her from falling and held her as I was reminded of the sadness from so long ago. It seemed I held her for a long time, though it might only have been a few minutes. As her other children were huddled around her, she was able to recover and she gave me another hug. She said, "Thank you for being here." Of course, I, too, had tears rolling down my face because for the last several minutes, I had been sharing in the stillness of my spirit, "Let it happen that she have peace."

Butch and Bobo's mom was absolutely one of the nicest people I've ever met. Through all the sadness she'd endured, she was somehow able to muster a smile as time went on and was able to be a real encouragement. I remember when I was wrestling at Marquette and I'd see her around the city, she would often initiate a conversation. When she asked how I was, she really wanted to know.

Exactly one week after Bobo's funeral, in the same church and the same cemetery with the same priest, I was at the funeral of my dad's sister, Francis. She was eighty-four years old. It's not often that funerals are happy events, but my Auntie Faye had been having health problems for quite a while and her husband had passed away eight years earlier, when he was eighty-three. If you had known my Auntie Faye, you would say she had a good run, which is my interpretation of a life well lived.

She was also very kind and I thought about my experiences of a week earlier during Auntie Faye's funeral and burial. In fact, her gravesite is thirty plots to the south of where Bobo was buried.

About three hours later, I was back at work. I had two appointments coming up that day and Lenore, my assistant at the time, came into my office. She asked what was going on and I said I was just at a funeral for my aunt. She asked how I was doing and I started to cry. I said, "I'm not really sure how it all works, but my aunt was eighty-four and Bobo was forty-two. Why do some live a long time and some go sooner? I had a high school friend named David who died at twenty-one. I'm just kind of curious about how it all works."

She said, "It sounds like you're going to make yourself crazy. I guess you can do that if you want to, but I don't ever really focus on how it all works. I guess I'm too busy with my little part of what my life is about and making sure that works."

That comment was just enough to shift me into thinking that I don't really need to know how it all works. I just know that I never got ahead thinking about my past.

MARATHON MAN

In 1980, one of my college friends told me he was going to run a marathon the next October, in 1981, the first Milwaukee Lakefront Marathon. He had competed in track in high school and was an avid runner.

I told him, "I can run a marathon, too."

He smiled and said, "I don't think so."

I said, "I think I can do it."

He said, "It's three to four hours and could be longer if you're not training."

He was expecting to finish in about three hours and fifteen minutes. He weighed about 140 pounds and was 5 foot, 10 inches. Obviously, being a gazelle, he could float right through a marathon.

I'm more of a Clydesdale, a big, heavy-footed horse, so needed a different strategy. I thought about it for a couple of days. The Marquette athletic program was very generous in providing for us for all the years we wrestled. However, some things were just not available, given their budget.

I set out to run the marathon and approached businesses and individuals I knew to raise money, and ended up raising several thousand dollars to support Marquette wrestling. The pledge was that if I didn't finish, the donors didn't have to pay. By the time race day arrived, I had just over $380/mile pledged for me to run the 26.2-mile event.

For me, it was not a race; it was a long, long run. Four hours and two minutes after I left the starting line, I was out of sugar, out of gas, and at the finish line. Remembering Al McGuire's words, that "proper planning prevents poor performance," helped me train for that momentous event.

I followed a training routine used by many marathoners: a longer run on one day and a shorter run the next. On the seventh day, I would do one long run consisting of half a

Marathon man?

Not at all, but ex-wrestler McGaver want to help MU's minor sports

By Mary Schmitt
of The Journal Staff

Fred McGaver knows that it is a pretty crazy idea.

"Like playing chess in a checkers tournament," he said.

But McGaver is a pretty crazy guy. Crazy, but dedicated. Always has been. That's what helped him become an All-American wrestler at Marquette University. And so when he says that he is going to run the Lakefront Marathon Sunday to raise money for the nonrevenue sports at Marquette, believe him.

"I'll run it, believe me, I'll run it," McGaver said. "It's a grueling event, I know. But I will finish. I'll walk part of the way, I'm sure. But I won't quit. I will not throw in the towel."

McGaver graduated from Marquette in 1980 with a degree in business. As a junior, he finished fifth in the heavyweight division at the National Collegiate Athletic Association tournament. As a senior, he was hampered by a broken foot for part of the season, but he was ranked 16th in the country and qualified for the NCAA tournament, where he lost in the second round.

Had to resign

Last season, he served as an assistant wrestling coach at Marquette, but he had to resign this season when he seized upon this crazy idea. NCAA rules prohibit coaches from being involved in fund raising.

And McGaver does intend to raise funds. Under the slogan, "Let's help this big man help small sports at Marquette," he is seeking sponsors to pledge money for each mile he completes in Saturday's race. He had a friend, Jim Finnerty, draw up a flyer and has distributed the flyers to Marquette alumni groups, and especially to those alumni who competed in minor sports at Marquette.

"As an assistant coach last year, I worked with a lot of recruiting," said McGaver, now an insurance agent for Northwestern Mutual Life. "And if you're trying to recruit with no money, like we were, it's just not going to happen. Marquette hasn't had a real fund raiser since I left.

"That's what prompted me to do this. We had to get some kind of fund raiser together. I think if I get to the right people, people will give. They just have to be approached."

"I'm just a guy who wants Marquette athletics to go somewhere. Marquette wrestling paid for a great portion of my schooling, and I want to give something back. It's not important that the money goes to wrestling. It will go toward helping all sports. And if you help one minor sport, you help them all."

The only sport that really won't be affected by McGaver's efforts will be basketball, but Coach Hank Raymonds, who also serves as the athletic director, has already sent a check for $25 to the Marquette Minutemen.

And Barney Karpfinger, the former Marquette wrestling coach, has pledged $15 a mile.

So far, McGaver figures to collect $1,100 in pledges if he finishes the marathon. But he would like to increase that total. He suggests that alumni can make a monetary sacrifice if he can make a physical one.

And it will be a sacrifice for McGaver. Those who know him say that he is more likely to talk a marathon than run one. At 5 feet 8 inches and 250 pounds, it is easy to understand why. McGaver understands it, too.

Ultimate challenge

"It's something totally out of my league," he says. "My anatomy is excellent for wrestling, but it's terrible for marathons. It's the ultimate challenge.

"I've read every book on marathons. I tried following their training schedule for a month, but I got burned out. They say to run 60 miles a week. I run about 35. I'm just not a distance runner. I have a Barney Rubble stride, a little, short stride.

"I have always done some running, though. I've been in good shape, as far as fitness goes, for the past four years. I've got good wind.

"I'll just be real steady, just as I was in wrestling. I'll need all the heart that I had in wrestling, too. I'll need all that persistence and will to keep going. I'm not looking for a good time. I'm just looking to get to the finish line.

"It's like I've been telling everybody who sponsors me or who makes fun of me. I'll see you at the finish line."

Those who would like to sponsor McGaver may call Frank Galka at (414) 276-4455.

—Journal Photo
Fred McGaver hopes to go 26 miles

Marathon Man?
Milwaukee Journal,
Sept. 17, 1981

marathon (thirteen to fourteen miles). I would then take one day off. I did this for three months.

When marathon day arrived, I was quietly confident at the starting line. This was different from wrestling. It wasn't about who was biggest and strongest, but about who would get to the finish line before the ribbon was taken down and the race closed.

About three weeks into the training, my adopted wrestling brother, Dan Jones, decided to get into the action and run the race, too. Sixteen miles into our race, he started to fall behind and told me to go ahead so he didn't ruin my pace. He finished forty-five minutes after I did. Of course, he had knee injuries from his wrestling days, so it was a pretty incredible feat for two crazy wrestlers.

The money we raised went to a special account at Marquette to support wrestling. The athletic department was able to buy things they hadn't been able to acquire in a while, like a new scale, some padding for the walls in the wrestling room, and some travel bags for the team's equipment.

I had been working in insurance for a couple of months. Don Schuenke, president of Northwestern Mutual at the time, happened to be a client of my manager, Herb. Herb mentioned to Don what I was doing and said, "Count me in," and Don pledged $50/mile. It was pretty amazing how some people stepped up to help me meet my goal.

Barney Karpfinger also committed $15/mile and sent me to a few of his business buddies, who also supported me. Another adopted wrestling brother, Frank Galka, pledged $10/mile. Back then, that was a big deal. I ended up raising just over $19,000. It just goes to show what you can do when you put your mind to it and you have the help and support of people like Dan Jones.

* * * *

Even though we all have limitations because of our circumstances, like our anatomy or different abilities, we can still challenge ourselves. I would not be bold enough to say I can do anything I want to do, but I can certainly challenge myself to do things that are out of the norm of what I would usually do. Such an accomplishment might even serve a purpose and be a foundation for you to achieve other milestones. From training for and running a marathon— something very different for a wrestler—I learned that it mattered very little what other people said to me.

What I tell myself is most important and, if you think about it, we all talk to ourselves through our thoughts all the time.

"OH, NO –
NOT WRESTLING!"

I magine that you've just started a new relationship and you're learning about each other. In the process of sharing your past paths, you tell your new sweetie about your sport or your passion. One day, I was talking to Toddy after we had been seeing more of each other for a couple of weeks. I told her that I'd wrestled and coached wrestling for many years. I'll never forget her reaction.

In a high-pitched voice, she exclaimed, "Oh, no, not wrestling!"

I asked her what that was about.

She said, "Wrestling?" with a frown on her face, like maybe tennis, cricket, or basketball, or something else would be acceptable, but not wrestling. I could feel the judgments that she had on the sport and possibly herself that she would have to tell other people in her life that she had recently begun to date a wrestler, with all the explaining that she felt obligated to do.

I meet people every day in my life who never wrestled and I never think any less of them. When I run across people who have mastered a musical instrument or excelled academically or in the sport of their passion, I must admit that I think of them differently, in a positive way. I explained to Toddy that several of my friends were incredibly successful, being teachers and business owners and doctors, dentists, and lawyers, and on and on.

There was something about that conversation that taught me that regardless of how good you are at something and how much it might mean to you, there are some people who will not understand or accept it because of their own judgments. Not only will discussing it not be neutral, it will be a negative experience for both parties. After that, I never talked with Toddy about any of my wrestling friends or lessons.

That was back in 1998. I worked as a volunteer wrestling coach and would go to wrestling matches and tournaments with the teams. After the events, I would stop to visit Toddy. I would never discuss whether we won or lost. We usually won. The new relationship reminded me of my upbringing in some ways, because as I got into wrestling, since my older brothers never participated in a sport, it seemed senseless to ask them what they thought about sports, because they hadn't experienced the sport or the competition. Obviously, the more Toddy and I got into the "Oh no, not wrestling," the more apparent it became to me that she was more concerned about image and the opinions of others than learning about that important aspect of my life.

When this happens, it doesn't mean the other person is a bad person. However, just be aware of it so you can protect yourself emotionally from sharing something that is incredibly important to you with someone who has no understanding of its value or that of the mentors who were key influences in your life. What I learned most from this experience was to ask more questions when I came across a person who had traveled a much different path than mine.

In his book *The Seven Habits of Highly Successful People*, Stephen Covey says, "Seek to understand." Wise counsel. I've found and continue to find that as I keep asking questions, the facts reveal that when I have a preconceived notion about anything, I'd made my first mistake.

It should be obvious that I had preconceived notions about Toddy, first because her name isn't really Toddy. "Toddy" is the name I gave her because she was raised in a privileged environment, attending and graduating from the best schools, and knowing from a young age that all was available to her without question. I would often kid with her about the Toddy name. She would call me "Toady." A "Toady" was definitely not as sophisticated as a "Toddy."

I've seen occasions where Toadies and Toddies do quite well together, but this will not happen when they hold their judgments near and dear, because, once again, judgments prevent you from seeing what's really there. When you judge anyone or any situation, you have to sit with that judgment until you let go of it. Once you let go of your judgment, you will begin to notice that the decision you made about the situation was actually you jumping conclusions without having all the facts.

IF YOU HAVE TO CRY, JUST CRY

My brother Joe told me about a house he bought when he lived on Wisconsin Avenue in Wauwatosa. The woman he bought the house from had lived there for the past fifty years. At the closing, with her daughter there, she asked if she could come back to the house one more time just to walk through it so she could say goodbye. He gave her a set of keys and told her to take as much time as she needed. He wanted to know when he could come by to do a few things. She said he could be there.

He said he had to run some errands and would be by in a couple of hours. When he arrived at the house, the daughter mentioned that they were just about done with the tour.

The elderly woman said to Joe, "I lived here for over fifty years. It was a wonderful house to live in. The neighbors were amazing people. I hope you live here a long time, too. Remember, though, *you really never get to keep anything. You just get to use it for a while.* I'm very thankful for how this house has served my family. When I came to this house, I was 28 years old and one of my grandchildren just turned 30 the other day." She then thanked Joe for allowing her to come back.

This leads me to my goodbye to a building I'd built. Although Toddy was fourteen years older than I was, when she met many of my friends, they often thought she was younger than me. Her physical attractiveness was only one aspect of her overall beauty, because she was amazingly versatile, with the schooling of a registered nurse and experience in nursing. She was an entrepreneur, developed real estate, and could learn almost anything. Even though when people met her, she would be very cheerful, kind and polite, I learned from her levels of intensity I didn't know were possible.

Around the time I was selling my business, I was also selling my building. My building initially started out as a 3,000 square foot warehouse, but I added on to it a couple of times and 3,000 square feet became 30,000 square feet, including another set of offices.

On one particular day, I was out of steam and Toddy said, "Let's go and work on your building," because I had to be out in two weeks. I was overwhelmed about where to start, so when we got there, Toddy took a few minutes to assess the situation, put together a list of the things we had to do, and then we developed a strategy for dealing with the list. It was clear she was telling me she was doing one thing and I was supposed to do something else. I appreciated that about her because I was all "decisioned out." "Decisioned out" is a Freddyism that describes when a person decides he doesn't want to decide anymore and starts living by default instead of design. This wasnn't a good place for me to be, but it was my place at that moment.

Toddy started working and I ended up moving some furniture to another part of the warehouse. I got distracted in the second set of offices. I sat in the conference room for a few minutes and remembered the many interviews, business meetings, and conferences I'd had there, and I decided to say goodbye to the room, as crazy as that sounds. A couple of minutes later, I went to the next office, then a minute later, I was in the next. About ten minutes later, I was sitting in my own office, which was at the end of a long hallway. I chose to sit in the window well and just reflect.

I then heard Toddy walk into the general office as she gave out a couple of "Yoo-hoos" in a high, cheerful voice. She got to the long hallway and saw me sitting there. She walked up to me and I said to her, "I was just saying goodbye to all the rooms." Then I started to sob. She stepped into me, hugged me, and held me as, I realized later, I must have been having a nervous breakdown on some levels.

For the next forty-five minutes, I just sobbed. She never said "Stop." She never said it was going to be okay. She never said a word, but I felt a sense of love from her that allowed me to totally express myself without any judgment. I am sure that environment was instrumental in me becoming complete with the emotional aspects of losing my business, an experience I was resisting.

After I seemed to recover, I thanked her for being there with me. I remember her telling me, "This is exactly where I need to be, too." I remember telling her it was time to turn off the lights and we would come back another time. I took her to dinner.

The last time I lost in wrestling, I felt sad and I cried for a long time, but I never felt as broken as I did that day with Toddy. As I look back, when I lost in wrestling, I lost in one aspect of my life. At that point, I had a successful insurance practice, a successful embroidery company, and other real estate holdings that were going along just fine. These other successes diluted the severity of my sadness at losing in the Olympic trials.

The worst thing about the loss of my friendship with Toddy is that have been many times after it ended that I wished she was around, because by then, I was more equipped to handle accepting love from her and to be more loving to her. I've also realized that if Toddy hadn't been in my life, I dread to think what would have happened because when everything was falling apart, she certainly demonstrated a deep sense of love and stability that I hadn't experienced before or since.

A few years later, I was talking to an undertaker who was a client of mine. He's a fourth-generation mortician. I asked if I could ask questions about his work. He was very open about it.

"What are the hardest funerals?"

He said, "Teenage auto accidents. The next hardest is young mothers. The next hardest is infants. The next hardest is young dads. The easiest ones are when they are close to one hundred years old and there are over one hundred descendants present. Those are the easy ones. There's one more that's really hard—suicides. When you do a funeral for a suicide, everyone's walking around with question marks on their foreheads. They don't see them, but I notice them. They're wondering why they're all there when they should be at work. We get to know the families very well in all these situations. The more severe the loss, the more extreme the emotional expression, which only makes sense."

He then went on to tell me, "What I think happens in the suicide situations is that people close different doors in their lives little by little before there is a physical suicide. You have to know that before the physical suicide, there was a spiritual suicide, then an emotional suicide, and then something just flipped or went wrong, and no one was there to get them through it. The difference is always having someone nearby or in your life, at least, who can help you get through those challenging times."

Then I told him my Toddy story, where she held me for forty-five minutes. He said, "Remember, I'm a mortician, not a psychologist, but that's a hell of a nervous breakdown and a healing process. You could well have had five years of therapy in fifty minutes. Lucky you that she was there." I agreed.

I don't care who you are or what you have or what has you, if you're going to feel something, you're going to feel happiness and you're going to feel sadness. We've all heard it—it's not what happens to you, it's how you handle what happens to you. Even though we've heard all the wonderful clichés, walking along the path of sadness is never a happy time.

One thing I've learned is that, no matter what feelings I've had—intense happiness or sadness—they're just feelings that flow through me. That awareness has helped me to be free to stay in the moment and not get stuck resisting a past unhappy experience or fantasizing or imagining a happier time.

If you're sad, cry.

If you're not sad, always smile.

And speaking of smiles, if you aren't wearing your smile as you walk out of the house each morning, you're not dressed to go out. A smile increases your "face value" one-thousand fold.

SAYING GOODBYE AND
JUST BEING THERE

I remember December 12, 2003, very clearly. I was in Hartford, Wisconsin, when my mother called me to tell me that Dad was having a hard time and asked me to get down there right away.

I was about forty miles away, and about forty minutes later, sat in a chair at the foot of his bed. Seated next to me, on the right, was my sister Christine. To the right of her was my eldest brother Charlie, and sitting in a chair at the side of my father's bed was my mother.

During the last few minutes of my father's life, he was very coherent and knew he was having a hard time, but I don't think he knew he was leaving the planet so soon. Over the course of an hour and a half, nurses kept coming into the room to see how they could help. He was running a fever and I remember he had a blanket over the slip-sheet keeping him warm.

After a short time, he said, "I'm too warm, take off the blanket." Then about fifteen minutes later, he asked to have his foot warmers taken off. In seconds, that was done.

Half an hour passed and he asked the nurse to take off the sheet and he was left with just the "johnnie," that garment patients wear to have something on while in a hospital bed. About two minutes after that sheet came off, he said, "Eleonore, some water, please." He took a sip and some dripped down his chin. My mother wiped it as it happened and then he said, "Eleonore, thank you." He never took another breath.

I said to everyone in the room "Hey, look, Daddy Mack just left. He left the planet." My mother checked his pulse. She kissed him and tears rolled down all our faces. I felt some sadness and much gratitude—gratitude that I got to witness this kind of love. It was incredible to be a part of and incredible to witness.

My father and mother were a great example of a couple who were very different, but focused on what they wanted to create together.

The senior nurse on staff came in, listened through the stethoscope for a minute, looked at the clock, and said to my mother, "Eleonore, I am so sorry."

Minutes after my father passed, my mother and my siblings were thanking the nursing staff at the Village Manor Park in West Allis, Wisconsin, when the nurse on staff (Kim), one of the key people, commented to my mother, "We have never seen so many members of a family come to visit any of our patients so often and so consistently. Eleonore, I know this is hard for you, but Frank was having a hard time for a long time. You gave him the best care anyone ever could have and we are thankful that we could be a part of it."

In one of her saddest times, it was nice for Mom to hear these words of encouragement. Sometimes, enough is enough.

UNSPOKEN EULOGY

My father's funeral took place five days after he passed on. Family discussions had resulted in a decision that no one from the family would give a eulogy. That was a hard decision for me to accept, for I had hoped for a celebration of my father's life, not an impersonal service performed by someone who hadn't really known him well. However, most of my family members wished for the priest to perform the entire service, so that was what happened and it turned out fine.

I gave a lot of thought to what I would have said in a tribute to my dad, and this is what I came up with. I'm sharing it here so that you can understand more about him.

"I am Freddy McGaver, the youngest of six children. I'd like to personally thank my mother, my brothers Charlie, Joseph, and Rick, and my sisters Maryann and Christine for allowing me to share this brief message with you.

On behalf of the family of Frank McGaver, we thank you for being here at this most difficult time for us as we honor the memory of our father and friend.

A kind word, a great sense of humor, a real sense of goodness would summarize my father's life. He was a model of what a husband and a father should be. He worked hard and always made time for us—from school projects to life projects. With my mother's help, we, the children of Frank McGaver, were truly blessed in every way a child can be blessed. Our parents were always there for each of us, regardless of our unique and different needs. As adults, our father became our friend and we were fortunate to be able to help take care of him and try to return a mere fraction of the countless favors he extended to us. He was always concerned with having our long-term approval over short-term approval, which often led him to be painfully blunt. He was usually right on.

Every day, regardless of how my father felt, he would say, 'Thank you.' Such a sensitive person is rare. Gratitude was part of who he was. All the people who extended care to him noticed how he was always in a state of contentment and gratitude. It is said, 'The richest of all people are those who are content.' My father was a very rich man: not measured in money or material wealth, but in goodness and in love.

My mother the warrior, a champion of life, is the best friend he ever had.

There is one story that I would like to share—how my father and I learned some wonderful life lessons together.

In June, my mother told me Father was feeling very sad. He was telling my mom he was afraid to die. When I went to visit him the next day, we had the most wonderful visit. Anyone who knows my mom would know that she was there.

I said to him that Mom had mentioned that he'd been a bit sad lately and I asked him what he was sad about. He said: "Oh, I would like to be able to walk again and get around. I would like to know that Mom and the kids and the grandkids will be fine. I would like that the kids could all get along and do well."

I then told him: "You have to know that Mom and all the kids and grandkids love you very much."

He said, "Yes, I know. It is nice. That is why I feel so sad sometimes. I see all the kids and grandkids helping us all the time, and I want to know that they will be okay. Saying goodbye makes me sad." And he started to cry.

Then I said, "What if, instead of saying goodbye each time people come to visit, you said something else like, "See you soon? How would that make you feel?"

He said it a few times and smiled. "Yes," he said, "that feels much better than 'goodbye'."

I told him about a meditation I'd recently been given and told him how it had helped me. The premise, simply put, is that what you give out, you get back. Knowing that you get what you give, you extend to others that which you want to have in your life. By blessing everyone, you will then be blessed by everyone. By extending peace to others, you will yourself have peace.

I asked him if he had regrets about his life that he wanted to talk about. He paused for a minute, and then he said, "Not much, really. I have been happy for a very long time. The only thing I regret is, at times, I hold on to things way too long."

"Like what?" I asked. He didn't say anything, but had a thoughtful expression on his face. So, I asked again, "Like what?"

This time he answered, "Like Sister Giles." Sister Giles was one of my father's sisters who served as a nun in a convent all of her adult life.

I asked what happened and he simply said that all that mattered was that he was upset at one time about something but he didn't need to hold on to it anymore.

I asked him if he thought that the meditation we talked about might be helpful to him. I encouraged him to say what he was sad about, focusing his attention on Sister Giles. We then said together, "Let it happen that everyone have peace."

I said, "Let's try it again." Then, the fourth time we said it, tears rolled down his face. I just held his hand, and we said it many more times together. He became more open each time he said it. At one point, a sense of peace came over him.

He looked at me and said: "This is really nice."

Then I asked him what he wanted to have happen.

He said, "I would like for everyone to get along."

"Dad," I said, "I'm sure that what is happening is you just put into motion a lot of healing. As we extend to others what we want, we create in our lives the very thing we give to others."

What he shared with me next took a long time. My father said to me: "I grew up poor, and we never had very many things. My mother was wonderful to me. My sisters helped me as I got older, but for a long time, I never knew what happiness really was. When I met your mother, Eleonore, my life changed that day."

We were both silent with our tears for several minutes. Then he said, "It was incredible. Her father was such a nice man, the kind of man you want to become, and her mother was so good to me! They really accepted me into their family. I never thought I was unhappy until I met your mother and found out what happiness was. Since then, I have been as happy as a man could possibly ever be."

Well, what happened next was just as amazing. The same night, after my visit with my father, my mother called Sister Giles, told her about my father's current condition and asked her if she would come to see him. Even at age ninety-six, she agreed to come soon.

The following Monday, Sister Giles came to visit. "Oh Frank, it is so good to see you! It is so good to see you!" They laughed and smiled through tears and shared old memories.

Then Sister Giles said, "Can you believe it, Frank? It is 2003 and we are the only two left." More tears. After several hours of visiting and healing, they thanked each other. Sister Giles held her brother's hands and told him again, "It is so good to see you, Frank!"

Eight days later, Sister Giles passed away.

The next Thursday afternoon, I went to visit my father. We shared a bond of a strong love without ever saying the word. As I left, he punched my fist gently as that was all he was able to move. With a soft smile and a sense of peace, he said to me, "You take care of yourself."

I said, "I'll see you soon."

My father replied very slowly, "Hey, Freddy! Let it happen that everyone have peace."

As I drove home that night, I cried all the way, knowing that my father was letting go.

The next morning, my mother called me and said that Dad had taken a turn for the worse. When I got there, Mom and my other siblings were sitting around his bed. They were keeping him comfortable.

When I walked in, Dad said, "Freddy!" I went up and touched his hand. Remembering so much of what we had shared, there was no need for words. Eventually, he started to feel warm. You could see he was letting go. Then he asked for more water. My mother held the straw to his mouth as she had done thousands of times before. He whispered a "thank you" and then he was off to be with God, the family he came from, and my mother's parents. He never did say "good-bye"... he said "thank you" to his best friend.

We sat there for about an hour, just reflecting, feeling everything, sharing our tears, sadness, a sense of peace and a whole lot of love.

We are thankful to be his children. The children of a union formed sixty years ago between a nurse and a worker, a nurse who healed an injury and a man who fell in love. The love that he gave is the love that he left with all of us.

In closing, my father asked me to share our special visit. He said I should tell everyone who would listen.

People don't need to wait so long to let go of things, especially when it's so easy to do.

I'm doing today what he asked me to do.

I would like to invite all of you to think of and say often as you live your lives, throughout your busy and sometimes troublesome days, my father's last words to me:

"LET IT HAPPEN THAT EVERYONE HAVE PEACE."

MY WRESTLING CAREER

Freddy wrestling (1974)

Pio Nono High School State Champions—Wrestling, 1972

Wisconsin Wrestling Club at the University of Northern Iowa celebrating a national team championship. Freddy McGaver is pictured on the left side of the front row.

WHY I STARTED TO WRESTLE

I wrestled in high school, first trying out in my junior year. I didn't go out before that because I didn't believe I could be good at it—so I didn't even try.

How I finally got involved was completely unforeseen. None of my three older brothers was an athlete, but my high school friend, Bill Hinkens, was a wrestler in high school. I delivered his paper route for him during the wrestling season.

When he was a junior, he lost a close match for the state championship title to a senior. Because of this, Bill was on a mission in his senior year. The senior who defeated him had graduated, but the defending state champion in the next lower weight class moved up a weight class for the state tournament. He had not lost a match in over two years and had a winning streak of forty-four straight matches. Bill had one loss that season and, because of a case of mononucleosis during the midseason, he missed a whole month of wrestling, but now was fully recovered and gearing up for the state title.

His high school team had four wrestlers who made it to the final round. He was one of four wrestlers who needed to win in order to clinch the team championship.

Bill's match was the first of the four matches and it was a big deal. He was going up against the defending champion. Bill won 6-2 in a match in which he dominated. This was an upset to anyone except those who knew Bill. Billy's team-mates won the other three matches and the team title was theirs.

After the match, people swarmed around Billy, offering their congratulations. I asked him if he heard me yelling in the stands. His response shocked me. He said, "I did not hear a thing." I didn't understand that. This was 1972, before "The Zone" was revealed in athletics. The "zone" is when everything falls into place and everything goes your way in a seemingly effortless flow.

It had been so exciting and I felt so drawn to the competition of the matches that I decided, that very day, that I wanted to wrestle next year. With my friend Paul Mulqueen, who was a freshman starter on the wrestling team, I began to work out that summer. His older brother, Mark, had been State Champion in 1967 and had earned All American status in college. He gave us large doses of reverse psychology almost daily. He taught us how to lift weights and took us under his wing. He would say, "When all things are equal in a match, the strongest man wins. Be the strongest guy!"

We got strong. At the age of 16, I weighed about 165 pounds and was bench-pressing 275 pounds, which was strong in those days. Although I had strength, I lacked technique. Mark would take us to Marquette University and we would work out with some of the college wrestlers and other high school kids in the open wrestling program being offered in the Milwaukee area in those days. Going there made me realize what a novice I was—that I did not have a clue about what was involved in becoming a good wrestler.

Every time I went down to Marquette, I would ask, "What did he do? How do I stop that? What should I do in this situation?" I caught on fast. It was important, remember—important! It was something I really wanted to do and to get good at. I was determined to do whatever I could, every day, to be better.

I was told that because I was coming out for wrestling as a junior, I would have trouble beating the other upper classmen. That fear drove me to work for hours on my conditioning. I would run the paths along Lake Michigan two to four times a week. There was a 75- to 90-second sprint up a steep service road from the lake. Then I'd jog back down and repeat the pattern eight to ten times. I ran often because the buzz was "endurance changes everything," and it did.

As a junior, I wrestled at 185 pounds in my first few matches, beating out a third-year wrestler, a junior, for a spot on the team. As the weeks went on, I was asked to go down to the 167-pound class to help the team.

Billy (Bill Hinkens) was an assistant coach on my senior team, and when I wrestled in the finals just two years after he won a state title, he cheered for me. As I walked off the mat after losing 9-8, I told him, "Thank you for pushing me and helping me. I heard everything you said." I was remembering what drew me to want to do this sport.

My entire senior year, I worked out with my friend, Paul Mulqueen, who was a junior and had his heart set on becoming a state champion. My senior year, I lost in the final match of the State Tournament. Earlier that night, Paul had lost to an outstanding wrestler from Marquette University High

School named John Hartwick. When those guys mixed it up, it was war. They were two great athletes who went all out the whole time. As things worked out, they wrestled the first match of their senior year in a dual meet. Paul avenged his loss by winning that match 14-5 as he dominated John. During the year, John dropped from the 167-pound class to 155-pound class, and at the end of the year, both won State Championship titles.

Paul became Thomas More High School's first undefeated State Champion. Both athletes are in their respective high schools' Halls of Fame. Often in sports, only one can win but there are no losers.

Paul Mulqueen winning another match. In 1975, he was the undefeated state champion.

After that year, Paul was recruited by several schools offering wrestling scholarships. He eventually accepted an athletic scholarship at Marquette University. Even without a scholarship, I tagged along to Marquette with Paul. I did not have the undefeated record to match the Paul's success, and was grateful to be on the team. About two weeks before the semester started, I was offered a sheet metal apprenticeship. I passed up that opportunity to pursue a college degree and continue competing. As things worked out, Paul decided in the middle of his second year that he did not want to compete any more and went into construction. Thirty-six years later,

Paul Mulqueen (left) and the author in 1998 outside Paul's house in Cudahy, Wisconsin.

he is still with the same company as a senior supervisor of many of the firm's biggest jobs.

Everything worked out perfectly for him and for me, too. Eventually, I earned an athletic scholarship. It was my good fortune to become Marquette's first All American and be inducted into the Marquette University Athletic Hall of Fame. There is no doubt in my mind that my high school coaches, Ron Fieber, Tom Knitter, and Bill Hinkens, along with my friends, Paul and Mark Mulqueen, were key people in my life to help me get to the next level, college wrestling.

Hinkens state finals, state champ 1972

I was still the shortest guy on the team, but with the help of some tough teammates and great coaches, we were State Champions. It was an honor to compete with these guys. I still know many of my peers from my high school wrestling team. Like Jesse Owens said, "The great friendships you make will last a lifetime."

The Thomas More High School wrestling team is pictured below. I am the shortest guy in the top row in the center. As a junior, my goal was to make the team and survive. With a lot of endurance, I discovered I could fit right in. Over the summer from my junior (my first year wrestling) to my senior year, I was able to become Team Captain and enjoy amazing success. I still believe if you train really hard the whole year, no matter what sport you are in, you can jump way ahead of those who just train their sport in that season. I still see wrestling shirts around that say "Summer Wrestlers are Winter Champions."

1972-73 Thomas More wrestling team (yearbook photo)

VARSITY-STANDING (L-R)-Bob Sweet, Paul Mulqueen, Mike Zaharias, Vince Kohne, Fred McGaver, Paul Beste, Jim Burns, Paul Podlaski, Steve Bejma. KNEELING- Dave Seitz, John Schneider, Jim Wurm, Mark Jendrzejek, John Vanlanen, Gerry Gates, Mark Kazmierski.

Doug Andrewski, Parkside

YOU CAN YELL AND SCREAM BUT IT WON'T MAKE A DIFFERENCE

Desiring things too strongly creates resistance. When I was a young coach just out of high school, I was sitting on the chair cheering for the wrestlers who had been underclassmen the year before. I yelled at them to stay in the match, keep on their opponents, grab an ankle or wrist, clear the arm, or do some other technique of our sport.

Then I would remember something about a particular wrestler, like he hadn't been at practice for two days that week, or hadn't really worked hard because he hadn't been focused, or perhaps he felt obligated to wrestle because an older brother had wrestled, or whatever. None of the reasons really mattered, but if I looked long enough, I would find a reason that the kid didn't seem to care.

I would often lose my voice screaming at these kids only to find that I had trouble with normal conversation because I had sacrificed my voice the day before by screaming at a kid who didn't really care. I had to come to accept the simple fact that just because *you* want something, doesn't mean someone else does. I concluded that sacrificing my voice was a foolish thing to do over a wrestler who wasn't committed to being his best. I let go of the belief that he had to do anything, which took away my resistance about him having to win.

OOS, OOG, OOB

When you compete in wrestling, it is you and your opponent. Coaches can encourage you. Friends can cheer. Family can support you. However, when you're out of sugar or out of oxygen, no pep talk will suffice to get you through the match. I often would tell kids I coached "OOS, OOG, OOB."

They would always ask, "What does that mean?"

I would respond with, "OOS is out of shape, OOG is out of gas, and if you meet the wrong opponent, you'll be out of business [OOB]." As I told wrestlers this over the years, I told myself the same thing.

I've said for years that problems never happen when they appear to happen, they only manifest at the time they seem to happen. I learned early in my wrestling career that I was so afraid to lose that I would work on my conditioning very hard to make sure fatigue wouldn't be a factor against my opponent. As I look back, I rarely lost because I ran out of gas [OOG] when I competed. I usually lost on technique, where the other guy was just better. I did not often lose based on my conditioning. Knowing this added to my confidence to go all out.

In high school, I learned that I could win most of my matches on strength alone, with a little bit of technique. In college, I could win on strength and technique, but needed to be well conditioned. On the world-class level, I had to have strength, technique, balance, endurance, and street smarts to win.

I remember reading a quote by Jesse Owens when I was still in college. Jesse was quoted in a book, *All That Glitters is Not Gold,* in which he talks about many of the experiences he had as a black athlete competing at a world-class level in the 1930s. At the very end of the book, it says, "The gold turns to green and the silver turns to gray and all that matters and all that you remember is the good friends you made and the good times you had."

I don't need to wait until the end of the book to tell you that. This idea sums up the rich life experiences we have when we are passionate about the process and not stuck on a goal as the only end. Not everyone can be the best, but we can all grow when we have a healthy focus and embrace the process of our path.

Coach Barney Karpfinger
(1976 Marquette University Yearbook)

BARNEY KARPFINGER

I met Barney Karpfinger when I was 16 years old and came to open wrestling at Marquette University with Paul and Mark Mulqueen. A usually soft-spoken guy, Barney had a way of talking that people listened to. In 1953, he was undefeated as a senior at Marquette, along with his teammate, Harlow Helstrom, who was also undefeated. Barney established Edgerton Contractors, an excavating firm, and at the time I met Barney in 1973, he was happily married and had eight children.

Each year the new basketball players would ask Coach McGuire, "Who's that gray-haired guy who is always walking around in the training room wearing a t-shirt that is drenched in sweat?" Coach Al would always respond, "Oh, that's Barney. He's the wrestling coach. Don't let the gray hair fool you. If you want to find out, go in the room and tell him how tough you are and he'll surprise you every time with how much more work you need to do."

Most years, that would be all that Al would have to say to his players, but sometimes he would get a second question: "What's the guy like?" To that, he would say, "I can summarize it real quickly for you. Barney Karpfinger is the kind of guy you want to become."

Regardless of how people encountered Barney—as an opposing coach, opposing wrestler, as a coach, or even as an athlete who would leave the program before graduation because he had different goals—they would all say they were treated with the greatest respect and also have the greatest respect possible for Barney. He was no doubt one of the most loving people you would ever meet.

Coach Larry O'Neil

LARRY O'NEIL

Larry O'Neil graduated from Milwaukee's Washington High School, and went on to study at UW-Madison. In his second year, he became a volunteer wrestling coach at Madison West High School and coached at various schools until 2006. I met Larry in 1973 as a high school junior when he was the assistant coach for Barney Karpfinger at Marquette University, which hosted open wrestling. Open wrestling was an opportunity athletes from the Milwaukee metropolitan area to work out with each other and some local college athletes. Larry coached from 1947 to 2007 at various schools. In November of 2007, Larry was on his way home from wrestling practice when he was involved in a tragic car accident and died five weeks later of complications.

Larry was one to gather lots of facts by listening. Once you got to know him, he was quick to show his great sense of humor. He would often joke around with us to soften the seriousness of intense upcoming matches. Once a match started, though, he was more focused than we were.

I wrestled in Wisconsin State Amateur Athletic Union wrestling tournaments in and after college from 1975 on. During my matches, he could be anywhere in the gymnasium and start saying, "Get motoring" or communicating some directive. There was something about his voice that you could hear throughout the gymnasium. It was similar to the voice of Burgess Meredith in *Rocky*, with a raspy tone. He also had the ability to turn up the volume quite loud. I would tune into his voice and it would put me into a zone of being right on schedule for another victory.

In wrestling matches, coaches for each wrestler sit on chairs next to the mat to offer advice and encouragement to their wrestlers. Larry was sitting on my chair in 1975; I was eighteen years old and won my first WI-AAU Championship. He was also there when I lost my last match at the 1996

Olympic Trials. He missed a couple of hundred matches in between, but somehow, he would often find a way to be at any local matches.

I don't know about other sports, but I can tell you that wrestling is an amazing fraternity. About a year after Larry passed away, I was at a restaurant with a group of people and was introduced to a musician named Tom McGirr, who was in his early sixties. Somehow, the topic of college sports came up and he mentioned that he wrestled. With an alert ear, I heard him say how wrestling had been really important in his life at that time because it taught him things he would not have learned any other way. I asked him which program he wrestled in and he responded the University of Wisconsin –Milwaukee. I asked what his team had been like then. He said they had a great team.

Tom proceeded to tell me that his coach was very instrumental to his finishing school because a couple of times he had been very close to leaving. Without the coach's help, he knows he would not have finished at that time.

"I had coaches just like that," I responded. "When that happens, you end up loving them forever." He then asked me where I wrestled and I told him Marquette University. He said they used to wrestle Marquette. He asked me who the coaches were and I said I had five coaches over my four years. The first two years, I was coached by Barney Karpfinger and Larry O'Neil, with Jerry Gradisnik and Frank Galka as volunteers. In my last two years, my coaches were Dan Jones, Mike Beining, and Bob Healy. His face lit up and he said, "Larry O'Neil is the guy who helped me get through college." I informed him that Larry had passed away the year before.

We ended up making a toast to Larry and agreed that there are hundreds of kids like us whom he impacted over his more than fifty-year coaching career. I would often tell kids who wrestled for me that when Larry O'Neil sat on your chair, he was completely on your side. It was like having five extra points before you even shook hands with your opponent. He'd work on you, he'd work on your opponent and orchestrate the circumstances so you would end up with the most points. He would find a way for each of us to find our own way to be and do our best.

IT ALL WORKS OUT

Larry O'Neil would often say to me: "Freddy, it all works out" whenever I talked to him about a problem. He would repeat what I just said to him and then he would say "It all works out." He would repeat what I just told him about what could go bad and would then say "It all works out."

The first time I got the lesson, I asked him, "How can it work out?"

He responded that even if it doesn't work out, it really works out. While Larry never said this directly, my conclusion was that he knew there was a higher path in place and then he would give me examples. Businesses sometimes don't work out. The people who scatter from the businesses are all provided for with new jobs, challenges, and new things to get excited about. Sometimes they go the other way, which is less beneficial, only to learn the new lesson to seek the new level. Often, relationships seem to blow up and even though they don't work out, they worked out because the people involved are now better equipped to avoid the mistakes if they have the maturity to go into the next experience and leave the baggage behind.

Regardless of your situation, of how it might not be working out the way you might want it to work out, just say the sentence, "It all works out." You'll find it always does.

MY DAD'S THANK YOU TO MY ADOPTED DADS

You know by now that two of my three "dads" were my former college wrestling coaches, Barney Karpfinger and Larry O'Neil. Both of them have been inducted into the Wisconsin Wrestling Hall of Fame and the USA Wrestling National Hall of Fame. They have been acknowledged and known as masters in our sport for a very long time.

Larry and Barney shared the following story with me about six months after my father passed away. Over the years, they often met my parents and me at different social functions. One day, when he was near Dad's nursing home, Larry went to see him. They had been visiting for a short time when a nurse came into the room.

My father said, "This is Larry. He's one of the guys who coached my son."

The nurse asked, "What did you coach him in?"

Larry responded, "His son was a wrestler."

The nurse asked, "How did he do as a wrestler?"

Larry said, "For over ten years, he was no doubt one of the top twenty wrestlers in the world. Even though he was never on the final Olympic team, he was consistently at a caliber where he could train with the very best."

My father then said, "I had no idea that he was that good! I always thought that when he was going to wrestle, there was just a bunch of guys in the room wrestling for the heck of it." Larry laughed.

When the nurse left the room, my father asked, "How did he get so good?"

Larry said, "I've been coaching for more than fifty years and I've seen very few people in any sport who work as hard as Freddy works. He would come earlier and stay longer than anyone else to perfect skills and build endurance. Many times, he would work so hard he would run his opponent ragged. It looked like the other guy just quit. For a big man, he is no doubt one of the quickest wrestlers I've ever seen."

My father shook his head in amazement at what he was hearing, and then he said to Larry, "For all the years Freddy wrestled, I would tell him that wrestling was a waste of time. I didn't have a clue of how good he had become." They chatted for a while longer and then Dad asked if Larry would come back again and bring Barney with him.

A few days later, Larry and Barney popped into Dad's room. After minutes of small talk, my father thanked them for coming and, although my father sat in a wheelchair, able to use only his left arm enough to raise it enough to touch your hand with his closed fist, his mind was as sharp as ever.

He said to Barney, "When Larry came by the other day, he explained to me how competitive Freddy was during his years of wrestling. I have to tell you, I had no idea how good he had become. I remember that when Freddy was only four or five years old, he was incredibly persistent and we had our hands full. I was very concerned about who he would associate with as he grew up."

My dad continued, "I guess every parent wants his child to make the best choices possible. I feel bad that I told Freddy that he was wasting his time. Now I realize how thankful I am that you were in his life! I couldn't teach him a thing about wrestling...and the value it brought to his life. I know that you two were incredible influences on his life and responsible for his attending Marquette and excelling in something so important to him. I never felt threatened or insecure in any way about the powerful influence it was obvious you had on him. But today, I want to tell you two guys 'thank you'."

Barney responded, "Over the years, we have coached probably a couple thousand kids and when a kid comes into the room with a work ethic like Freddy's, that gives us a lot to work with. Larry and I would chuckle, knowing that Freddy would wear out this opponent, too. Thank you for sending us a kid with a such great work ethic."

After that day, my father would introduce me to the nurses and medical staff, "This is my son, Freddy. He's a wrestler." This was my father's way to apologize for years of not understanding his son's passion for competition.

REAL EDUCATION: NEVER LET YOUR SCHOOLING INTERFERE WITH YOUR EDUCATION

As Mark Twain shared long ago, "*Schooling* is society's system of teaching one how to get along in that community. *Education* is life experience. Never let your schooling interfere with your education." I learned to interpret this as meaning that school is society's system to become learned, to exist, and to eventually prosper in that society.

Education, on the other hand, is made up of life experiences. While I felt school was important, I realized early in life that there were other important lessons to be learned in areas other than the classroom. Both places and modalities of learning are very important and helpful to anyone's growth.

DAN JONES

I met Dan Jones in the summer of 1973 at open wrestling. At that time, he was a varsity wrestler at 190 pounds for Marquette. I later connected with Dan in 1978, when Barney Karpfinger picked him to be the next head coach. Throughout his collegiate wrestling career, Dan was well respected as an athlete and team leader. He served as the head coach at Marquette for six seasons. Mike Beining and Bob Healy were his assistant coaches for his first two years.

I first met Dan Jones when I was a junior in high school and went to work out at Marquette University with the college team. At the end of one of the team workouts, Coach Barney Karpfinger let some of the high school kids work in with some of the college kids.

I got to wrestle Dan Jones. Dan Jones is 6 foot 6 inches and wrestled at 190 pounds. I was 5 foot 9 inches and wrestled at 180 pounds. In high school, Dan was a State Champion for Pius IX High School. In fact, when he was in

Dan Jones
with family,
2010

high school, he had to win his match in order for the team to win the state title. Talk about extra incentive. Dan was a two-time qualifier for the National Collegiate Athletic Association (NCAA) Division I tournament and had the opportunity to beat some really good wrestlers. When he got to wrestle me for the first time, I'm sure he thought it was a field day because not only did I not score any points, but when we did wrestle, he had me on my back most of the time, which is not the place you want to be in a wrestling match.

A lesson for young wrestlers is a formula I figured out a long time ago. If you have the height, then use moves that take advantage of your leverage because levers never get tired. If you have good leverage, you can break a guy who is really strong. I was pretty strong for a high school kid, but not strong enough to score any points. It was funny, because when I wrestled Dan Jones, I didn't know anything about him, like that he was a State Champion or had gone to the NCAA Division I tournament the year before. These things don't come up when you're about to work out with the team. For me, he was just a tall college kid.

Fast forward to spring of 1978. Barney Karpfinger and Larry O'Neil decided to retire and passed the coaching baton to Dan Jones and Mike Beining. I remembered meeting Dan several times since that workout at various Marquette wrestling events, but we hadn't had the chance to wrestle after our first meeting, which had been a pretty intense beating for me. Dan and I met for lunch one day with Larry, Barney, and Mike Beining. Barney explained that Dan and Mike were the new coaches, but that he and Larry would both still be around to see how we were doing. They were not going to check up on Dan or Mike because they had total confidence in them. I told Barney and Larry how disappointed I was that they were stepping down and Barney said, "We all need to be open to the idea that our lives are constantly changing. I am open that mine is, too, because for twenty-three years, this has been a big part of my life."

His telling me that he had been coaching longer than I'd been living at that point, it was obvious that I could not understand there are different phases in each person's life and that Barney and Larry were ready to move to the next phases of their lives. Larry continued to tell me, "Since you first walked in the room and struggled to get down to 177 pounds, and since you're now over 250 pounds, it's obvious that you need someone who can push you physically and Dan will push you," and he smiled.

I felt a nervous prickle when Barney asked if I'd ever worked out with Dan before. I told them what happened when Dan and I first wrestled. Larry smiled and said, "That will happen again." At the conclusion of our visit, Barney said, "Don't think of it as losing two head coaches. Think of it as getting two more." After that visit, I had a lot of peace about what was coming up because I had a deep respect for all four of those men in different ways.

Over the summer, a few things started to happen. My top priority was healing from my knee surgeries. Second, Dan Jones and several other wrestlers decided to have a testimonial dinner for Barney Karpfinger.

In October, 1978, more than 400 people from all over the country came to the Pfister Hotel in Milwaukee to salute Barney for his 23 years of service to Marquette University. In the process, I became the "go-fer," helping to do a lot of the detail work for the dinner, like the mailings, putting together a list of all the former wrestlers, getting the addresses, phone numbers, and so on. That was before the Internet and meant a lot of phone book work. I spent a lot of time in the library and working with alumni staff at Marquette University to get the information.

The testimonial dinner was successful and actually very easy to put together because of the great respect so many people had for Barney. This was also good for Dan and me because the first thing we worked on together was successful.

After expenses had been paid, we used the extra money raised by the event to send Barney and his entire family to the 1980 Moscow Olympics. However, because of the boycott (the US teams did not participate because the USSR had invaded Afghanistan), Barney asked if he could use the money to take his whole family to Austria to connect with relatives he'd never met before. When he got back, he told us what a great time it had been. He had taken his parents, who were in their eighties at the time, as well as his children, to the Old Country.

Dan was big on having the wrestlers run at the beginning of each wrestling practice, where a lot of coaches might not be. He would run us hard at the beginning of each practice before we even got to wrestling. Having competed for Tom Knitter, I was familiar with this because Tom would also run us ragged. We were always in very good condition because of this. Another part of the training was instruction on moves and live wrestling (all-out exertion).

Because there wasn't another heavyweight, my partner was often Dan. Three years had gone by since we first wrestled, when he pummeled me. I'd also packed on sixty pounds, mostly muscle. Although he would beat me on the mat, it wasn't as lopsided as it was the first time we had tangled. Having Dan to wrestle with every day was invaluable for me because I learned different techniques that would help me beat a taller guy.

After a couple of weeks, Dan said he learned something, too. He would recruit former wrestlers from the area who were still in pretty good shape to come work out with me. The advantage was that I had many partners to work out with on a given day. I would stay in the center of the mat and they would throw me a fresh guy. Although many of these wrestlers were competitive, I would usually do better. One thing they did do for me was help me work hard, which increased my conditioning.

My practice was typically made up of about three-minute, all-out efforts with a few seconds' break between different wrestling partners. These would go on for about an hour. The last thirty minutes, when I was out of steam, Dan would start working in and he would be one of my three-minute guys. It was much more even, then, and there were some days he would really hammer on me.

Dan Jones taught me how to be tough on the mat. That was his specialty. The joke on the team, when he wrestled, was that he would always be taken down in the first few seconds and the earlier he was taken down, the bigger the mistake it was for the guy who took him down. Many times, as he was on the way to the mat, Dan would reverse his opponent and end up on top. Once he got on top, you were not getting out. The pressure was amazing. Remember, leverage doesn't get tired. Muscle does.

As I mentioned before, and I will again, there were many people involved in my success as a Marquette wrestler, but if I had to point to only one person, it would be Dan Jones.

Workout partners I had included Dan Ackman, Tom Burns, Frank Galka, Ben Guido, Bob Healy, Joe McCook, Ray Jacobson, Mark Krenek, John LaPlante, Keith LaPlante, Ben Peterson, Grady Sagorak, Joe Schuster, Laurent Soucie, Larry O'Neil, Michael O'Neil (brother of Dan O'Neil and son of Larry), and many others.

What was interesting about training with all those guys, except for Laurent Soucie and Ben Peterson, was that no one else was competing. They were doing it to help me. In all the years I competed, I had a sense of stewardship about my training partners. I would be tough, but never take cheap shots or do anything that could hurt them. Even today, when I'm asked about high school or college wrestling, I tell people that it breeds a lot of respect.

I also felt an extra responsibility when I was wrestling to really go all out the entire time so their efforts were not wasted. I would often be in matches where there would be a little crowd in some of the small gyms we would encounter. I would think about my training partners and really motor.

"Motor" is a Larryism. Larry would tell us right before a match that it was time to get motoring.

Dan Jones is one of my adopted brothers, along with Frank Galka. These guys were a big part of my life during my college days. They helped me become the best I could be and are some of the closest friends I have today. Another by-product of wrestling, intertwined with the deep respect for one another, is the incredibly deep friendships that can endure a lifetime.

From left to right: Freddy McGaver, Dan Jones, Barney Karpfinger, Larry O'Neil, Tom Knitter, and Mike Beining at the 1999 Marquette Athletics Hall of Fame induction ceremony.

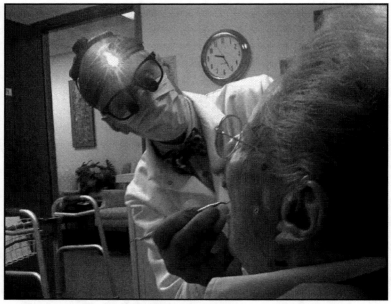

Frank Galka, DDS. Frank has been practicing dentistry on Milwaukee's East side since 1973.

FRANK GALKA

Frank Galka was a high school wrestler at Marquette High School and college wrestler at Marquette University from 1964 through 1969, so he was ten years older than me. He was a volunteer assistant coach for many years after graduation while he attended dental school, and at the end of the program in 2000, he was a key contributor to Marquette wrestling in every way a person could contribute. His hard work ethic and quiet confidence had a powerful impact on anyone who had the good fortune to be around him.

Frank Galka, another of my adopted brothers, was also a coach to me in my early years of college. Although in his wrestling he was incredibly intense and focused, in his life he's amazingly balanced. What I learned from Frank is enough to make a book in itself. One thing I learned early on from him is that, outside the wrestling room, the only thing that should be taken to an extreme is moderation.

If you met Frank, you would see in seconds that he is one of the most sensitive and caring people you will ever encounter. He's been a dentist since 1973. I have many dentists as my own clients, but he is *my* dentist. I've asked him over the years if he likes dentistry, because I've found that some dentists don't actually like practicing dentistry (as is true of many people in all occupations).

As a side note, it is surprising how many people in a wide variety of occupations truly don't like their work. They thought they liked what they did for a living and may have for a while, but have evolved.

Frank, though, says every time, "I love what I do and although I have to come in to my office and they call it work, the way I'm able to help people, many times it doesn't feel like work."

Frank is also a testimony to the idea that "like attracts like." If you meet his staff, they are all incredibly kind people. Frank is another person, like Barney Karpfinger and Dan Jones, who has taught me to not react quickly. Be aware of what's going on, but don't get emotional or demonstrate an emotional response.

That type of restraint has helped me avoid many misunderstandings over the years, where my ego would kick in and create a whole different outcome because I wasn't patient enough or diligent enough in observing the situation, and in turn, allowed things to get out of hand. I continue to strive to emulate the qualities I've learned over the years.

RON FIEBER

Ron Fieber was an accomplished football player at Marquette University and also a highly competitive boxer. Ron grew up in a house across the street from where I did—eighteen years ahead of me. His parents and mine were good friends. Ron coached high school wrestling and taught academics at Don Bosco and Thomas More high schools. He has since retired and lives in Colorado.

Perfect Practice Makes Perfect.

Ron Fieber was my first wrestling coach at Thomas More. While Coach Fieber never wrestled, he was a master of teaching details. He was a very good boxer at Marquette University in his college days. He taught me how to switch from the bottom position to the top position. He had our team do the moves so many times we could probably have done them in our sleep. That's where I learned that repetition is the mother of skill.

There were occasional whispers from some of the students who were "jacked up" (disciplined aggressively) by Mr. Fieber. He was very good at letting the students know what he needed them to do and convincing them to do it.

Although he never competed in wrestling, he applied many of the training principles he learned in other sports to wrestling to make sure we were well conditioned. Of all my coaches, he was one of the most intense. I remember him showing the team, when I was a junior in high school, a series of wrestling moves called a side-roll series. Because I was in the 170-pound range, he would often work with me to demonstrate moves to the team.

On one particular day, we practiced the moves and then we did live wrestling with our workout partners. Since I didn't have a partner that day, he worked with me and sure enough, he tried a roll; I had just learned the countermove, gave it a try, and he ended up breaking a couple of ribs. He was carried out of the wrestling room on a stretcher by paramedics. The next day, his mother, who was in her mid-70s, was talking to my mother and asked, "What did your son do to my son?" The conversation was more of an update on his condition than an uncomfortable confrontation because we all understood that it had just been an accident.

Within two weeks, he was back to wrestling with the kids again and it seemed to be business as usual. There were some things about Ron Feiber's intensity that were non-negotiable and he was extremely particular about the smallest of details. Even though he was never a wrestler, he took the time to master certain moves that he deemed useful for high school wrestlers.

One day, I came from behind and won a match. I was down seven points and after the match, he told me, "You won that match because of your conditioning. When I boxed, my conditioning was top notch and you have to know that your conditioning is exceptional. Make sure you go all-out right away in a match to use that advantage."

That conversation created a bond: Coach Fieber believed I could go the distance and I then started believing it more, too. It's amazing how positive and negative thoughts can feed off each other. He was an incredibly optimistic influence for me in many ways.

Schools were different when I was young and our private school allowed even a bit more freedom to discipline students than was allowed in the public schools. Even in our current climate of political correctness and preventing any child from failing at anything, sometimes a "tune up" is exactly what is needed.

Very few students would challenge Mr. Fieber more than once. While he was usually very kind, he could also be tough if he felt that was what the student needed to be successful. For me, he was a great motivator and I found him to be a man who personified strength and gentleness.

Coach Ron Fieber shouting at one of his athletes in 1973.

TOM KNITTER

Tom Knitter was a social studies teacher, as well as being in charge of the audio-visual department at Pio Nono High School. After the merger of Pio Nono with Don Bosco in 1972, the school was renamed St. Thomas More High School. Tom eventually served as principal of Thomas More, and later as the school's president, and was instrumental in the school's becoming a nationally acclaimed Blue Ribbon School. He is now retired, but still helps out at Thomas More in various capacities.

"The only thing you can't do is you can't say 'you can't.'"

In high school, I enjoyed a lot of success because of my conditioning alone. However, to become one of the top wrestlers in my league, it was important to add more moves to my little bag of tricks.

My senior year, my coach was Tom Knitter. He had been the assistant coach for several years and, although he never wrestled himself, he was a master at coaching and communicating details. He could motivate the kids at every level, from the kids who were soft and needed special handling to the kids who had an attitude and needed to be tuned up. He could adjust accordingly and make it all work.

One day, we were practicing a new takedown and I had trouble learning the move over the course of the hour that we had been practicing it. When he came around and I was doing a different move, he asked why I wasn't doing the move we were working on. I said I couldn't do the move. He asked why I couldn't do the move. I shook my head and said I couldn't do it. He said, "The only thing you can't do is you can't say you can't."

He made me repeat the sentence, "The only thing I can't do is say I can't," and had me repeat it about six times. I tried the move again and he had me say the sentence again.

After twenty more attempts at the move and twenty more repetitions of the sentence, I was beginning to understand the move. The move became ingrained in me over the next several weeks. It was this move that allowed me to win a tight match and put me into the state finals a few weeks later. "You can't say you can't. Say something else, but don't say you can't."

Coach Tom Knitter, Thomas More High School, 1974, during the state finals.

Tom Knitter was my high school coach and a social studies teacher who eventually became the principal of Thomas More High School, as well as the president of the school. Like many private schools, tough decisions have to be made and those who are aware of the history of Thomas More and the struggles they endured agreed that the correct, prudent, bold decisions that Tom Knitter made are some of the reasons the school still exists today.

* * * *

This photo of Tom Knitter and Olympic wrestling champion Bruce Baumgartner was taken when Bruce came to speak at a Marquette University wrestling alumni event in the late 1990s, in front of Thomas More High School.

While Tom and Bruce are both very competitive in their own ways, they are no doubt two of the nicest people I have ever met.

Bruce Baumgartner and I competed against each other when he was a student at Indiana State University and I was at Marquette University. Bruce went on to become the most decorated American wrestler in the history of our sport, winning two Olympic gold medals, one Olympic silver medal, and one Olympic bronze medal.

* * * *

Bruce Baumgartner came to speak at a Marquette University wrestling alumni event in the late 1990s. I picked Bruce up at the airport and as we drove to downtown Milwaukee, I asked him whether he wanted the scenic or the direct route. He asked what the scenic route was and I told him it would take us by my high school. He opted for the scenic route. It was 5:15 on a Saturday afternoon. As we drove by the high school, I noticed Coach Knitter's car there. We walked into the front door and there he was, working at his desk.

I introduced Bruce to my coach and my coach said, "I thought that was you" because Bruce is a legend in the sport. What an honor it was for me to have one of my first mentors in the sport of wrestling meet one of my last mentors on my path in the sport. As we drove away, Bruce commented, "It's no surprise that a guy like that would be running the school because it's Saturday night and he's still working there. That guy must be really committed to making it work." I then shared with Bruce some of the tough decisions that had to be made and were made. It was really inspiring to be able to take the picture of two champions along my path.

MIKE BEINING

Mike Beining was a three-time state champion while attending Pius X High School in Milwaukee. In his college days at Marquette University from 1971 through 1975, he was also very successful. Mike was assistant coach to Dan Jones for the 1979-1980 season.

"When you shake hands with a guy and the whistle blows, what are you thinking—and what are you going to do?"

This leads me to focus. One day, Mike Beining, one of my college coaches and himself a three-time high school state champion, asked me, "When you shake hands with a guy and the whistle blows, what are you thinking?" I remember telling him that I was open to seeing what might happen.

He then asked, "Do you have a move or a strategy in mind?"

At that point, I often did not and told him so. I asked him, "When you shook hands, what was your strategy?"

He said, "Well, that's easy. I'm was going to get after him and wanted to do everything I could do during the match to break my opponent's will so I could score the points I needed. Whether it was one point or ten points, I would approach it with all my attention on that move, like it was the only thing I had to do. When that was done, I was into the next moment, focusing on the next moment of what I had to do. When you approach a match that way, you never look at the clock, your opponent is usually spent because you outworked him, and sometimes you are amazed that the match is already over."

What I learned from Mike was to approach each move like it's the only thing you have to do today and then get on to the next thing you have to do. Coach Larry O'Neil, one of my adopted dads, would also say, "Just do the next thing."

Keep in mind that Larry has also been one of Mike Beining's wrestling coaches when Mike was in college. You don't have to think too long to figure out where Mike's approach came from, or may at least have been fine-tuned.

I have found that it is okay to approach things with incredible intensity and focus, and although it works very well in a wrestling match, this approach needs to be softened in other applications in your life. I have learned and am still learning to temper my approach and intensity because sometimes people don't appreciate my focus. I guess this is more evidence that an attraction can be a distraction or an asset can be a liability, if not balanced.

BOB HEALY

Bob Healy was a high school state champion for Francis Jordan High School in 1969. In his college days at Marquette, he was known for his intensity and endurance. Even though he only weighed 160 pounds, he would wrestle anyone in the room. Bob was the son of Howard Healy, one of my college professors. He was one of my coaches from 1979 to 1980.

"Wrestle a full match" - keep going all out until the final buzzer regardless of what the score is.

Many people have commented over the years that pound for pound, Bob Healy was one of the toughest, best-conditioned athletes to ever go through the program, and who has great knowledge and passion for the sport. When I was a senior at 240 pounds, Bob Healy weighed 160 pounds. There were many times, in a two-minute drill, that I could not get out from under his pressure. He taught me how to maximize pressure on my opponent like few wrestlers I've ever encountered. It was amazing to have a father and son coach me about school and wrestling, while they were really teaching me important life lessons.

Bob Healy, celebrating one of his many victories as a Marquette University wrestler from 1969 to 1974.

CHAMPIONS AND FRIENDS:

RUSS HELLICKSON, BEN PETERSON, LAURENT SOUCIE, BRUCE BAUMGARTNER, RULON GARDNER, AND DAN CHAID

In wrestling, not everyone can win,
but there are no losers.

In 1978, I had the opportunity to wrestle a guy named Ben Peterson, who happened to be an Olympic champion in 1972 and a silver-medalist in 1976. It was at the Midlands Tournament at Northwestern University in Evanston, Illinois, by many considered the toughest amateur wresting tournament in the country. I lost to Peterson 9-3. A score of 9-3 might not seem to be too bad. However, when you consider that I only scored one of the three points because the other two were awarded when he let me go only so he could take me down again, it doesn't look so good.

Because that was my fourth year as a wrestler (two years of high school and two years of college), I looked at it as a victory in many ways, because with his skill level and my lack of experience, it could have been a lot more lopsided.

After the match, I remember telling my coach, Barney Karpfinger, that my neck was trashed and I wouldn't be able to go on. He got me a couple bags of ice, had me go up in the bleachers and lean against the wall at the top of the bleachers with the ice wrapped around my neck and supported by a towel. He said, smiling, "You can be sore right now, but in

The author (L) training with Bruce Baumgartner at the University of Pennsylvania-Edinboro, 1996.

about 60 minutes, you have another match, so don't get too comfortable." He often knew when we could do more and challenged us accordingly; if we were really hurt, he was very sensitive about getting us the best care available. I wrestled in about an hour, won a very tight match, and my neck was not sore.

I wrestled another match and won. Then I had to wrestle another close match, which I lost to a guy from Iowa who had been a runner-up in the national tournament the year before.

What I learned from that match was that I had to focus on every moment I was in the match. The other wrestler's technique was superior and his pressure was so intense that to even attempt to neutralize his pressure, I had to be right there mentally so that I could physically resist his attempts to improve his position.

After my last match, I went over to Ben Peterson and asked him if I could talk to him for a few minutes because I wanted to learn what he was doing in a certain move when he had me on the mat and was trying to turn me on my back. He said he had to get ready for his next match and would rather take a few minutes after the match. After his match was over, he received his tournament trophy and mat card. (A "mat card" is the sheet posted on the wall for all the wrestlers to see who they wrestle throughout the day on the pairing brackets. The winner gets to take the mat card home.) He said he had to leave to go to Watertown because his ride was leaving in a few minutes. He gave me his phone number and said to call him on Tuesday morning and we would figure out a time to meet. We did.

On Tuesday afternoon at 3:00 p.m., I was in Watertown, Wisconsin at Maranatha Baptist Bible College. For me, it was like going back fifty years, even though I was only in my early twenties. The campus of the small college housed most of the students and had dress codes, like neckties and skirts and sport coats. Not knowing of the dress code, I showed up in a polo shirt, so did not comply with the student dress code. People obviously knew I wasn't a part of their school, but were amazingly kind as they all greeted me.

That afternoon, Ben and I were able to work out for about an hour and he showed me the move he used on me that had trashed my neck. That session began a friendship

Ben Peterson wrestling with Laurent Soucie at the 1980 Olympic Team Trials. The author trained hundreds of hours with both champions in preparation for his Olympic matches.

that would change my wrestling career and take me to levels I never initially thought possible. Over the next couple of months, we worked out two to three times per week for about ninety minutes, sometimes with another person working out with us. Through Ben's mentoring, I learned confidence, position, and new levels perseverance from a wrestler who, in many ways, was who I wanted to become.

It was not until my ninth workout with him that I scored my first takedown. I often drove the sixty-five miles from Watertown back to Cudahy, many times out of sugar and sore all over, with a heart of gratitude that I got to train with one of the best in the world. Even as a young man, I was amazed at what a kind person he was.

I continued to train with Ben through the Olympic trials of 1980, where he again was the top member of the 1980 Olympic team. Because of working out with him, I was invited to some of his other circles. This included an opportunity to work out with University of Wisconsin-Madison assistant wresting coach, Russ Hellickson, who was a silver medalist in 1976, and Ben's brother, John Peterson, also an Olympic champion in 1976 and a silver medalist in 1972.

When working out with them over the course of a couple of months, we would work in a circle, with the person who won each match staying in the center until he lost. I remember one time I got to stay in the middle of the circle for forty-eight minutes. It was the only time that ever happened because sometimes I would win once or twice and then be knocked off by the next guy coming in. That day I was on and they might have been off, but whatever happened, I

Ben Peterson (l), Olympic Gold medalist, 1972, Silver medalist, 1976, Olympic team member, 1980, the author, and Russ Hellickson (Olympic Silver medalist, 1976, Olympic team captain and team member, 1980. These two champions were the best mentors anyone could have for becoming a good wrestler and a great person. Both Ben and Russ are inductees in the U.S. Wrestling National Hall of Fame.

remember that workout with more pride than many matches because of who these people were in a sport I wanted to master.

* * * *

The sport of wrestling seems to breed much respect. The best wrestlers in the world, no matter what their situations, always have a sense of humility, knowing that if they don't keep their focus, they can easily end up on the wrong side of a contest. It generates a mutual respect from the highest weight class to the lowest weight class of athletes achieving their own excellence so that there are many champions. I also learned that by participating in a sport like this, not everyone wins, but there are no losers.

It's interesting to me, as I watch other sports and all the showboating after a basket or a touchdown is made, to see that somehow these athletes think that they really did something, when there are many more players on the court or the field who contributed to the success of the play. It seems to me that the tradition of wrestling is still the same in that you shake hands at the beginning of the match, you mix it up, and then you shake hands a second time. You may have an expression of excitement about your victory, but it is done in a respectful, kind, considerate, manner because there is a good chance you might be wrestling that guy again. We all know in sports that anything can happen on any given day.

* * * *

As I got to work out in Madison and practice with Russ Hellickson, I discovered in him a friend who was willing to help anybody (even though I was a Marquette student and could not benefit the Wisconsin program in any way) who would obviously invest the time and energy to improve himself to become better at the sport.

Over the next several years, I trained with the Wisconsin Wrestling Club and competed as the club's heavyweight, while Russ Hellickson encouraged me to become better. As I look back, all my mentors taught more than just how to be a good wrestler: they taught about the importance of being "good people." Russ Hellickson certainly personified that truth.

* * * *

In 1994, as I committed to train full time to make the 1996 Olympic team, I was able to work with Dan Chaid, who happens to be a former member of several World and Olympic teams, as well as an NCAA Champion. As a University of Oklahoma wrestler, he has the best win-loss record of anyone to go through the program. It was a wonderful experience to train with Dan because he is good at many things. He has several hobbies, a wide range of music preferences, and is a very good communicator, which makes him an exceptional ambassador for our sport.

One day, after one of our workouts, we went to a restaurant to get a bite to eat and Dan pulled out an appointment book. He said, "Okay, Freddy, let's get our schedules together for the next six months." In the next few minutes, we agreed to meet in various places around the country to train over the next six months. There are many things I appreciate about Dan; as a workout partner, with me weighing more than 280 pounds and him weighing 225 pounds, he was very hard to score points against. There were many times we worked out in rooms all over the country for an hour to an hour and a half of straight wrestling and we had the room to ourselves. At the end of the workout, there would be puddles of sweat on the mats. We would then move to another part of the room and continue wrestling.

I was always grateful for Dan's insights because he was very disciplined, quietly intense, and very willing to help others improve as he taught me some of the finer points of freestyle wrestling.

DON'T TAKE SHORTCUTS

O ne of my professors in business and management at Marquette was Howard Healy. I had to go see him at the end of the semester to learn what my grade would be for the class. I went to his office thinking I would show up and he would open his book to tell me my grade.

He asked me what I thought my grade should be. Not being ready for the question and remembering how savvy Professor Healy was, I stood there speechless for a few seconds. After I regrouped, I gave him a couple of answers. I would have liked to have an A so that it could boost my grade point. For the work I had done that semester, I thought he would give me a B.

He opened his grade book, pointed to my name and said, "Yup, you got a B." He then asked me if I was in a hurry because I was standing in the doorway of his office.

I said, "No, I just wanted to be brief and not take up too much of your time."

He responded, "I would also like to be brief, but if you are open to it, I'd like to share with you a few insights that I learned about you. Are you open?"

I said, "Sure," thinking he was going to say good things about me. He then proceeded to tell me that in the course of a couple semesters, he can get to know people very well, like you get to know your family members. However, over the years, he had come to have a pretty good idea what people were about.

"The good thing is you are getting a B. The truth is that if you had done a little more poorly on your final exam, it could have become a C. The sad thing is that it should have been an A. I notice that you take shortcuts. If I can help you with anything and you can really learn this today, learn that the shortcuts will kill you. Many people are able to get through life with talent only. That can be a blessing or a curse. The blessing is he gets a lot of things done easily, but only to a certain level. The curse is when talent gets a person to a higher level, but that person's lack of discipline prevents him from staying there." I was stunned into silence.

He continued. "McGaver, let go of the short cuts. You are a smart guy and, for years, I have seen smart guys who are not disciplined get only so far and fall off the track. Don't be a guy who does shortcuts. When you go the extra mile and spend more time learning things more deeply, whatever you do, you are investing in yourself. Don't do shortcuts."

I have to say that even today I occasionally think about my conversation with Howard Healy. I will be in a hurry, want to do a shortcut, and think to myself that I only want to take the shortcut this one time. I usually don't do it.

About a week later, in the summer before my junior year, I decided that because I didn't have great wrestling technique, I would have to make up for it in the areas of strength and conditioning. I decided that every other day, I would put my hands on the floor with my feet on a chair and do push-ups (an exercise where you push your body up from the floor) for one set until I couldn't do any more and then I would wrestle. I would run five quarter-mile sprints before and after each workout, no matter how I felt.

I did this for several years. Many days, when I would think about not doing it, I would remember vividly my lesson from Howard Healy, "McGaver, you're a talented guy, but don't give in to the shortcuts. The shortcuts will kill you every time."

Like many other teachers and coaches over the years, it is amazing how often their teachings still guide your life, how their words will resonate in your mind, even though they are no longer around.

Howard Healy passed away several years ago and I remember calling Barney, one of my "dads," to tell him about the funeral. I then drove over to his house and we went to the funeral together. He told me that Howard Healy was a great guy for everyone he taught because he wouldn't tiptoe. He taught several of our wrestlers and he not only challenged them to be better in the classroom, but also in other areas of their lives. I then told Barney the story you just read. He smiled.

GET THE BALL
IN THE HOOP

One day, I was working out in the wrestling room at Marquette University about hour before practice with Scott Grudzinski, whom I knew from another school in the Milwaukee area. We were both working out for an upcoming tournament and each had to cut some serious weight. When I was a freshman at Marquette, I wrestled at 177 pounds, which was a challenging weight for me to maintain (my average weight was around 210).

Scotty was a state champion from Milwaukee Juneau High School, and now was a freshman at another college and getting ready for a tournament. We jumped rope for five minutes at a time and took one minute off, for a total of twenty-five minutes of rope jumping.

Just as we finished, in came Al McGuire. He slammed the door and then slid his back against the wall, eventually going to the floor and wrapping his arms around his knees. He apparently hadn't realized that anyone else was in the room when he first walked in. It was only after he had been sitting a few seconds that he realized Scott and I were there, as we had the lights on only in the far section.

I decided to take a break and catch my breath. At the time, final exams were coming up. At midterms, I had a D in one of my classes. I had to decide over the next two days whether I was going to drop the class or try my luck at bringing it up to a C.

I asked Coach McGuire, "Hey, Coach, can I ask a question?" and he said, "You already did. What is your next question?"

"What is the trick to getting through this place?"

He replied, "I don't know. I never went to school here. I don't know a thing about it. What I do know is I have fifteen idiots upstairs who know everything about basketball. One guy wants to take a twenty-five foot bunny shot. Another guy says 'Throw it to me, throw it to me. Let me shoot.' Another guy wants to throw it through the hoop like a piece of paper in a wastebasket and another guy wants to run around the other guys and bounce the ball."

"Sometimes you have to get a tutor, sometimes you have to come in early and stay late, sometimes you have to ask for help, sometimes you have to do extra credit, sometimes you have to kiss a little butt. I don't know what you have to do, but I do know that sometimes you have to bounce the ball to get it closer to hoop. Sometimes the bunny shot can win the game, and sometimes…"

Then he stood up and said, "Hey, kid, I don't know what you have to do; just get the ball in the hoop," and then more intensely and loudly as he moved his hands at chest level and chopped the air. With each chop, he said one word at a time, "Get the ball in the hoop. Just get the ball in the hoop. Just get the ball in the hoop."

When he left and started walking down the hall, he was still moving his hands and saying, "Get the ball in the hoop!"

About twenty minutes later, I went down to the training room and told Bob Weingard what had happened.

Weingard told me, "Coach Al announced his retirement today and when he came in to the building, there were reporters upstairs. He just had a press conference at noon, told reporters that he needed to work with his team, and would appreciate it if they would not come around. So when he got there, he said, "Either you leave or I will" and he went down to the dressing room to hide as Sam Cook, the custodian, got everybody who was not associated with the team out of the building. After about ten minutes, he went back upstairs and got to work."

When I finished telling Bob Weingard the story, he said, "There is a good chance you did more for Coach Al than he did for you. Sometimes we need a place to go to just to clear our heads so we can refocus."

For several years, I often thought about "getting the ball in the hoop." It might have been get the leg, get the arm, get the hand, get your step, and on and on. It was a great lesson for me to learn to really focus.

Years later, fifteen years after the fact, I was telling some high school wrestlers about the story of when Coach Al told me to "get the ball in the hoop." I'd forgotten that somebody else had been in the room with me. Scotty, who was coaching with me, told me that he had also been in the gym that day. Sometimes, when Scotty and I were coaching and it was crunch time for one of our wrestlers, he would say, "Hey, Professor, it's time to get the ball in the hoop," and we would laugh about the lesson we'd learned long ago.

I am sure I've thought about Coach McGuire's words every month since I first heard them.

Marquette University basketball coach, Al McGuire

Al McGuire statue in the lobby of the Al McGuire Center, Milwaukee, Wisconsin.

AL MCGUIRE

**The Five Ps of everything are:
Proper Planning Prevents Poor Performance.**

I remember Al McGuire telling a basketball player in the training room about the Five Ps of everything. The basketball player was giving Coach Al some excuses about why he would not be on time for practice the next day. It was obvious that this player's appeal was not resonating with Coach Al. When the player was all done with his litany of excuses, Coach Al said, "The Five Ps of everything are: Proper Planning Prevents Poor Performance. I look forward to seeing you on time tomorrow." He then walked out of the room.

"HEY, BARNEY! DON'T MAKE SO MUCH NOISE!"

My second year at Marquette, I talked head basketball coach, Al McGuire, into letting me run on the track before and after wrestling practice. It didn't happen every day, but I would do this often. On one occasion, I was really tired because I would do four-lap sprints, which was equivalent to one-third of a mile. I would do five sprints before practice and five after practice on those days. From my high school days, I found that running before practice was really important for getting my body warm and avoiding injury.

On one occasion, I was tired and my feet pounded on the floor, my breathing was labored from doing sprints, and Coach Al yelled up, with his East Coast accent, "Hey, Barney! You're making too much noise!"

I thought he was saying "Barney" because I was one of Barney Karpfinger's wrestlers. The next day, when we were all in the training room, I found out that Al had actually been referring to me.

To Bob Weingard, the Marquette University athletic trainer, Coach Al said, "Hey, Buff, there's Barney," as he noticed me on the training table getting my ankles wrapped.

Bob said, "That's not Barney, that's Fred."

Al replied, shaking his head, "Nope, that's Barney. He looks like Barney Rubble when he runs around the track with his short stride." The deal with Coach Al was that I could only do sprints if I'd won the previous match or tournament. If I didn't win, I couldn't come up and run until I won again. I had to get in and out without making a lot of noise. I told Coach Al it should be just the opposite. He said, "You just keep winning, Barney, and we won't have to have this discussion." He walked away.

Marquette gym, with balcony running track on second level.

YOU GET A LITTLE BETTER EACH DAY

As a freshman at Marquette University, because of habits learned from Tom Knitter and Bill Hinkens, two of my high school coaches, I would run at least twenty-five minutes every day before practice, and could usually cover three miles in that time. Although many of my teammates in college did not run, I decided that I needed to run because I was well aware of the benefits to my conditioning.

The track coach at the time was Melvin Shimek, but those who knew him would call him "Bus" Shimek. I don't know how he got the name, but I do know that he was well respected and was instrumental in the success of the Marquette track team over a span of 50 years, from when he became the first All-American in track in 1927.

"Bus" was kind to everyone he met. He would often talk to those of us on the wrestling team. One day, when I was up on the track and his runners were coming upstairs to the balcony, which contains the track, I had just finished running and introduced myself to him.

He then said, "I noticed you've been here every day this week." It was a Thursday and he said, which I'll never forget, "Every day you come, you get a little better and every day you don't come, you go in the other direction. Coming every day keeps you going in the right direction."

I used to think often about his comments on the days that I didn't want to run because I just wasn't up to it or I just didn't feel like it and I would make sure that I got started and got moving in the right direction.

Melvin "Bus" Shilmek

DON'T GET SCORED ON

One of the first things you learn in wrestling is how to avoid getting scored on. Until you learn this, it is unlikely that you will be able to score on other people. You have to stop your opponent's offense with a successful defense so that you can implement your own offense.

Those who are involved in combat sports have a credo, "The best defense is a good offense." In wrestling, the best defense is a defense quickly converted to an offense. You have to stop the other person's aggression.

As the years have passed, I've learned that we get scored on in all kinds of ways. The most common is when we over-react. We go off on a tangent without enough facts. We worry about things that will never happen. We complain about things we apparently do not want to change or can't change, and all the while we're being scored on. When you react, you get scored on and often lose.

DON'T QUIT

I was a teenager when I committed this poem to memory.

When things go wrong, as they sometimes will
When the road you're trudging seems all uphill
When the funds are low and the debts are high
And you want to smile, but you have to sigh
When care is pressing you down a bit
Rest if you must, but don't you quit.

Life is queer with its twists and turns
As every one of us sometimes learns
And many a fellow turns about
When he might have won, had he stuck it out.
Don't give up though the pace seems slow
You may succeed with another blow.

Often the goal is nearer than
It seems to a faint and faltering man;
Often the struggler has given up
When he might have captured the victor's cup;
And he learned too late when the night came down
How close he was to the golden crown.

Success is failure turned inside out
The silver tint of the clouds of doubt
And you never can tell how close you are
It may be near when it seems afar;
So stick to the fight when you're hardest hit
It's when things seem worst that you mustn't quit.

— Author Unknown

YOU CAN'T
QUIT TODAY

Our focus is our future.

O nce I was in the training room at Marquette University, talking to the trainer about quitting wrestling as a freshman. Al McGuire popped into the room and the athletic trainer, Bob Weingard, said, "Hey, Coach Al, Freddy McGaver is thinking about quitting wrestling."

Coach Al said, "If you're going to quit, I guess you're going to quit. The great failure in life is not going out and losing, it's not going out at all." Then he left.

Bob smiled and said, "It looks like you can't quit today, Freddy, so get dressed and get back in the room."

Maybe there are times you feel like you want to quit, are resigned, like you've had enough, that it's just not worth it—whatever *it* is. I've had all those conversations with myself and still hear them from time to time.

Doubts and fears are also judgments your make against yourself. These judgments are not you, just thoughts and feelings that flow through your awareness. When you notice that you're having doubts or fears, perhaps acknowledging that they're just "doubts and fears" is all you need to shift you from that place of uncertainty to a place of refocusing.

Over the years, I've discovered that fears, feelings, and doubts are not me. When I identify that, I'm free to refocus on whatever I want to create. I invite you to learn how I have grown and to learn how you can grow by keeping your focus.

WE ALL GET TO LEARN DIFFERENT THINGS

Usually, during the first few days of a practice season, when I am talking to the team as a group, I will somehow explain to them that we get to learn different things.

"You will learn a lot about wrestling, because that's what I'll be sharing with you. Eventually, you'll learn more about life. As I watch you learn, I get to learn deeper lessons. My lessons may come in how to handle things that may happen—referees making bad calls, students or athletes not being respectful of others or themselves, parents not being able to support the athletes emotionally, or parents putting too much pressure on their children to win. All of these are factors in converting what could be an okay season into a great season." Or variations on that theme.

Remember, whatever you are doing in your life, whether you are learning or teaching, everyone gets to learn different stuff, but only if they're open to learning new stuff. Look for your openness and be aware whether others are open, as well, because they can have an impact on you—sometimes negative, hopefully positive.

MOTIVATION VERSUS MANIPULATION

A few times when I was coaching in events and we were in a tight match or tournament, the kids were aware of the team scores and they would feel pressure to perform. They would say, "You want me to win so you win, Coach."

Whenever this happened in my later years of competition, I would repeat their sentence to clarify that I heard it right, and I would say, "I've already won. I have a pile of trophies and a jar of medals at home from the many tournaments I've won. If you win or don't win, it won't add to my jar. Could it be that you're feeling nervous about what's coming up? Could it be an extension or a reflection of your preparation?"

As the conversation developed, I would tell them, "Whatever you do, you do for you." I would also reinforce the fact that they could add to their own piles of medals.

Do you know the difference between motivation and manipulation? Motivation is win-win, while manipulation is win-lose, often leading to lose-lose.

Those young athletes were trying to convince me that I was pressuring them to perform, but they didn't like the pressure. My response: "There is no pressure. Just go out and lose."

Whenever I said that, I could see their competitive sides start to shine through with more intensity. They would realize that they had worked far too hard to go out there and lose. Their focus would shift from being manipulated to a high gear of being extremely motivated and the blame game was over. It was amazing how they became motivated by shifting their focus. It would usually work out just fine.

HE WHO DOESN'T KNOW
THAT HE DOESN'T KNOW

I've often had wrestlers come to me, like I went to my coaches, with a crazy idea for doing a fancy new move. As I pursued new moves, I learned the importance of humility and practicing and drilling the move hundreds of times before attempting it in a critical situation. When athletes came to me with wild ideas, it was obvious I had rein them in like my coaches had with me.

Instead of discussing the move or what they were doing, which I initially found counterproductive, I would ask them if they ever heard the proverb, "He who knows that he knows is wise. Follow him." They always said no, they never heard of it. I would get a piece of paper, give the athletes a pen, and have them print it out for themselves so they could keep it.

I would tell the students that if they put me in their classes on Monday, I would quickly demonstrate that I didn't know that I didn't know. Maybe if I sat there long enough, I would begin to remember some of the things I'd learned before and be awakened and realize I do remember some of it.

I told students that when it comes to wrestling, I know that I know. For them to integrate such a strategy late in the season is very risky, especially when we consider that they had mastered move A, move B, and move C. To add something now is a bit risky. Of course, it was still their decision. They would usually agree to go back to the drawing board, which meant to drilling the move many, many times to increase their skill level and comfort level in executing it. When match day came, the mastered basics would prove to be the most successful strategy.

It is really important for everyone to know who they're talking to. If someone is giving a person advice about any area of life, it's also vital to grasp that the person they're talking to really knows about that aspect of life.

Now you know that "he who knows that he knows is wise." Follow him.

He who doesn't know that he doesn't know
is a fool—shun him;
He who doesn't know that he knows,
is asleep—wake him.
He who knows that he doesn't know
is a child—teach him.
He who knows that he knows,
is wise—follow him.

—Persian Proverb

SEVENTEEN DAYS

College was not only an awakening about what was required to succeed academically, but like starting over athletically. During my high school days, I enjoyed a lot of success right from the start. I lost to only four different people in sixty matches. Moves that worked a year or two before were somehow obsolete in college. It sometimes felt like I had completely forgotten how to wrestle.

At one point during my freshman college season, my record was three wins to eight losses, which was not on a pace to match my previous achievements. Coupled with getting hammered in the wrestling room more often, I was also getting more nicks and bruises. It's amazing how when you win a contest by one point, you have a lot of energy to get up and celebrate and how when you lose the same contest by one point, you're so exhausted you can barely move. It was definitely a time in my life when I lost by a single point again and again and again.

Of course, I had some options. The first one was to quit and the second was to work harder. The problem was that I had to completely retool, so where should I start? As I did my soul searching, I remembered one of my volunteer coaches, a former Marquette wrestler, Jerry Gradisnik, who had spent several days working with me one-on-one my freshman year of high school, teaching me how to set up a move and how to read my opponent so I could initiate a move without being overexposed.

Working with Jerry was very helpful to me in many ways because at age 18, I had never looked at wrestling as requiring a strategy before. I looked at it as a controlled fight. Wrestling does not involve kicking, biting, or scratching. You're not supposed to break bones or rip the extremities off your opponent, but it is a fight.

At Marquette, I began to realize that wrestling was an art, a martial art.

Looking back at turning points in my career, I recall at least twenty people who picked me up at one point and either pushed me, walked with me, or dragged me along to get me to the next level. Jerry Gradisnik caught me at a most fragile point because I was really close to quitting. Every day, I would go home from practice with at least three bags of ice. The ice would go on whatever hurt the most—ankles, knees, elbows—the ritual was twenty minutes on and forty minutes off, repeated three times. The next day I would feel pretty good and able to work out again.

I was learning how to learn. I remember reading a sign, on a wrestling room wall: "You are either the hammer or the anvil." In those early days at Marquette, I was definitely the anvil, getting pounded every day.

One day in late January, I went into the coach's office after practice and talked to Coach O'Neil and Coach Barney Karpfinger while they were both getting cleaned up to go home. I asked them if I could talk to them for a few minutes and that I would be brief. I said that I wanted to quit and wanted to thank them for all their help.

Coach Barney said, "Well, sit down a second and let me hear what is going on." Then I started to cry. Tears, great big ones, ran down my face and every emotion I could possibly feel seemed to be coming out: sadness, inadequacy, the regret of not being able to have a winning record, the low self-esteem of not feeling good enough. It was all there.

Barney asked what the problem was. I responded that it had been seventeen days in a row that I hadn't been able to get a takedown in the wrestling room.

Coach Larry piped up, with a smile in his voice, "Well, that's one hell of a slump."

Barney then asked what I was going to do and I said I was going to quit. He said, "You can't do that. You have to get on a winning streak and then quit on your own terms. It's really important that you quit on your own terms and that you don't get run out of town, because every time you hear about Marquette wrestling, see Marquette's logo, or anything about Marquette, it could trigger more sadness and more regret. The problem you have now is that you're in the club and you're having trouble."

Larry said, "Well, you know, Barney, even I've been hammering on him lately. Maybe he might want to quit."

It was amazing how, when I think back to what Larry said in a lighthearted way with a smile in his voice and how Barney behaved as if every word I said was serious and he took it seriously, he would bring Larry back to being serious. I was definitely getting worked by a good cop/bad cop routine.

Barney then said, "Hey, Larry, I have an idea. Where's the schedule for our meets?"

Larry, being incredibly organized, said, "Right here, Coach. In two weeks, we have the Wheaton Invitational at Wheaton College in Illinois. We've been successful there sometimes, but other years, we've had several individuals do very well in the tournament, but not enough guys to bring us enough points to win the whole tournament. If you can get down to 177 pounds in the next sixteen days, you could beat the two guys at 177 pounds right now in the wrestle-off and represent Marquette. If you win a match or two, or more, everything that you do will help the team."

He then continued, "Well, Tubby, what do you weigh right now."

I said, "I weighed in at 193 pounds."

"What will you weigh out at?"

"Probably 186 pounds," I muttered.

Then Larry said, "That shouldn't be too hard a cut if you start today. It's really important that you keep the fluids in your body and let go of the sugar and really work on the 'push away'."

"What's the 'push away'?" I asked.

Larry said, "Well, you know what push-ups are. 'Push away' is the push away from the table. If you can do that, you can make the weight. Now, what can we do to get you a takedown so you can enjoy some success?"

Barney piped up and said, "Larry, let's worry about that tomorrow." Then he looked at me. "Fred, can you give us two more weeks and then after the tournament, you can quit?"

After Barney and Larry had spun me around what felt like a hundred times, completely shifted me from tears to a new goal, addressed all of my concerns with seriousness and humor, I walked out the door, focused on being the 177-pound wrestler from Marquette University.

Fast forward two weeks to the Wheaton Invitational. Because Larry and Barney both had families (Larry had five children and Barney had eight children), along with their work and their commitments to coaching wrestling, their schedules were very full. On the day of a meet, we would gather at Marquette University and work out as a team. At the end of the workout, everyone would check his weight.

The day of the tournament arrived and we headed down to Wheaton. The coaches usually took two cars. I remember we had a flat on the way down. In typical Barney style, we didn't have enough air in the spare tire, so we had to go to a gas station to get the tire fixed and put air in it before we could replace the flat tire. We jacked up the car, took off the tire, and a teammate of mine, Paul Mulqueen, and I ran-rolled the tire for the next mile. I hadn't eaten in a couple of days, having only taken on fluid, and was getting dehydrated from working up an intense sweat. We got to the gas station, the guy popped out the nail, put in a plug, the plug held, and he took us back to the vehicle in his pickup truck. In a short time, we were back on the road.

We got to the weigh in, when all wrestlers have to step on the scale, and we were only an hour late. The officials at Wheaton agreed to let us weigh in, but we only got one chance because our team had been late to the weigh-in. I got on the scale and weighed 176.9 pounds. Had I not worked out before and run that mile, I wouldn't have made weight on the first pass.

The Wheaton pairing brackets came out and I had a preliminary round match. I had to wrestle a guy who was "fifth seed" in the pretournament rankings.

Let me explain the "seed" concept. In tournaments, the wrestlers with the top two or three records, or "seeds," are identified. The tournament director ranks wrestlers according to their records of wins and losses, and aims to keep the number-one person, who is called the "top seed," away from the number-two person, who is called the "second seed," so they can meet in the finals. Otherwise, you can have the first two seeds meet in the first round and end up with someone who is less skilled with a poorer record getting to the finals.

My weight class had several wrestlers with outstanding records and, of course, with me having a 3-8 record, everyone had a better record than I did. I ended up winning my first match 8-6 in a "barnburner," a tight match in which there was a lot of flopping around.

In the next round, I wrestled an unseeded wrestler and won 10-2. That got me to the final eight. In that match, I wrestled the third seed. His record was 26 wins and four losses. I knew I was in trouble in that one.

Right before the match, Larry O'Neil pulled me aside and got right in my face. He asked me what I was going to do. He said, "You should chase him and chase him and chase him and run him ragged. I was just showing you before how to stop his arm drag by keeping your thumbs in the armpits.

After your match, I pointed him out to you and said 'Don't let him fool you that he's better that you because he may have more muscle,' because when you move and move and keep moving, muscle gets tired and your endurance is really good. So, we're going to focus on pushing the guy and your endurance."

Six minutes went by. I got five points and he had two. I made the semifinals and had to wrestle the second seed, who had a record of 28-2. I thought my number was up. Larry said, "This guy is a master of the leg ride, so we're not doing leg rides today. We're going to be closing the knees together and as soon as he tries to put the leg in, do a sit out, which you've been drilling every day."

My opponent did indeed try to put the leg in, I did the sit out and was back on my feet. I won the match 8-4.

Incidentally, Frank Galka, a volunteer coach at Marquette at that time, would work with me on mat wrestling. He was exceptional at the leg rides and would teach me how to counter them. That proved to be instrumental in me winning that match. As the match unfolded and I was put in that position, all was familiar and I knew exactly how to counter my opponent.

In the finals, the guy I had to wrestle had a 30-1 record. Interestingly, the longer the tournament went on, because I was winning the tight matches, nothing was sore. My elbow, knee, and ankle injuries seemed to be gone because my focus was on the moment I was in. The final match started off with me being taken down right away. After about a minute, I got out. The period ended in a score of 2-1.

During the second period, I was on top and I rode the guy the whole period. The third period, I was down and got out.

Larry was always great. He'd pull me aside and say, "Just do this," in a raspy voice, then he'd get right in my face and tell me what to do. It was like being programmed as some kind of warrior to do your next assignment. He would say, "For the first minute, don't worry about getting out. Just don't get caught stalling and keep on working. When there is a minute left, I'm going to be on you and you have to get out right away and keep on chasing this guy.'' With 55 seconds to go, I got out and Larry was on me to keep on chasing him and chasing him. With ten seconds left, I got a takedown (2 points) and ended up winning the match 4-2.

You could not believe how happy I was to have a 7-8 record, which I would have scoffed at during high school wrestling. I got a trophy and the match card with all the names for all the matches of the event at my weight class.

At the Wheaton Tournament, the people are absolutely amazing. It's unlike most other tournaments because the students are instrumental in running the tournament and they're just really nice people. I don't say "really nice people" too often, but after I just beat their best guy and as I was walking by, their coach, Pete Wilson, congratulated me on a great match.

* * * *

Pete Wilson was a legendary coach at Wheaton College and when they had a fiftieth celebration of the Wheaton Tournament, I attended the event with Barney. Long after Barney retired from wrestling, he heard about this tournament and invited me to accompany him and Larry to express his appreciation for coach Pete Wilson because he was a great coach and a really wonderful person. Coach Wilson was an incredibly kind man, who was always gracious, regardless of the outcome or his team's performance.

I remember Barney telling me several stories about Pete Wilson's actions in seeding meetings, where they determine the rankings of the wrestlers. Coaches would get into arguments and he would let it the discussion go on for a couple of minutes, then he would state some fact about one of the wrestlers, and the argument would be resolved in a few seconds. Everyone respected Coach Pete Wilson.

* * * *

After the Wheaton tournament, we stopped at a Ponderosa Steak House, our favorite. We ended up in Glen Ellen, Illinois, for a late dinner. We were heading back to Milwaukee and sometime after 11:00 p.m., Barney had dropped everyone off except me.

I was sitting in the front seat and Barney said, "On Monday, I have some stuff to do in Madison, so I won't be there. Can you come by around 4:30 p.m. to drop off your equipment?"

I said, "What do you mean, drop off the equipment?"

He said, "Now that the tournament is over and you won, you can quit."

I just shook my head and smiled and said, "Barney, you are really goooooood." I was hooked again.

Barney said as he shook my hand, "I've coached for a long time. Your performance in the last two days is one of the most inspiring things I've seen in coaching, considering what your record was and the records you beat. Hopefully, you can keep building on this to do bigger things."

That weekend was a really turning point for me because I learned that records are just numbers on paper, and that when you shake hands with someone, which is how wrestling matches start, everything each of you has done before is irrelevant to what is going to happen in the upcoming match.

By the way, every time a wrestling match starts and ends, the two opponents shake hands. These handshakes are really important. The intention behind these handshakes is never explained to wrestlers. When you and your opponent shake hands the first time, you are giving one another permission to initiate a controlled fight within the rules, like *en garde* in fencing. After the match, the second handshake is an agreement to "leave it on the mat," including any unresolved conflicts. Wrestling tournaments always involve several periods and the wrestlers will be walking by each other as they prepare for their upcoming matches. Demonstrating such restraint is a key element in the mutual respect for one another generated within our sport. When people hear "wrestling," they are often drawn to the image of the nonsense they see on TV; real wrestling is all about learning and living respect.

WE LOSE OR WIN, A LITTLE BIT AT A TIME

L ooking back, I should have competed at Marquette throughout 1978, rather than helping out coaching at Thomas More. As I learned by reading books on codependency, the enabler of a person with an addiction, such as alcohol, will focus on helping the other person as a way to avoid working on himself or herself.

Anyway, there I was, working out a different brand of codependency: helping other kids win when, in some ways, I had given up on myself. Earlier that year, my knees were both injured, one knee when I fell off a motorcycle, the other playing tag football. One knee would act up when I ran with a full stride. The other had a sharp pain when I put too much weight on it, for example, when lifting another person. These were real injuries that gave me real excuses.

To make matters worse, one of my college teammates died tragically that year. Larry, Barney, another teammate of mine, and I went to Connecticut to attend the funeral.

On the way back from the funeral, I sat next to Barney on the plane. As we were getting settled, there was small talk. The conversation quickly evolved into my plans for wrestling the following year. I explained to Barney that my knees were injured and that I wasn't going to wrestle anymore. He agreed that it's hard to wrestle when you're hurt and that sometimes an injury can end a career. He also said that sometimes, with good therapy and medical attention, a lot can be restored, including knees.

Then Barney asked me, "If your knees were 100 percent, would you be more likely to keep wrestling?"

I said, "Probably," while thinking that I didn't know if I could get in that good of shape again.

He asked, "What has to happen for you to get your knees fixed?"

I mentioned that I'd spoken with the trainer and that it would take about two months to get on the schedule, which would put me at the end of June. Following eight weeks of therapy meant the end of August. College wrestling started two months later, in October, and I wasn't sure I'd be strong enough by then, so I didn't know if participating in the next season would be possible.

He then asked, "What other obstacles stand in the way of you wrestling this fall?"

"I need to make money to pay for tuition."

Barney nodded in an understanding way and asked, "Are there any other obstacles?"

I said I needed some spending money and as I worked out the numbers in my head, I told him I could get by on $50 per week.

Then he said, "If that were taken care of, what other obstacles do you have?"

I said, "There's really nothing else."

He asked which knee was less seriously injured. I told him my left knee. We were both quiet for a couple of minutes and then he said, "I coached a guy a few years ago who is now an orthopedic surgeon. His name is Larry Foster. Larry is a great doctor and a really nice person. I'm happy to consider him a friend. When we get off the plane and we get home, I'll call him. I don't know anything about his situation, other than that he might be on vacation, but if he's in town, you'll be having surgery next week on the less injured knee. Hopefully, four weeks later, you can do the second knee, which will give you plenty of time to recover before the season. Regarding tuition, if you promise to get in the best shape of your life, your tuition will be taken care of. Regarding your spending money, you're on your own, but I'm sure you can figure that out. That's not a factor; you can get what you need."

He then put his hand out to me at chest level and said, "Do we have a deal?"

"A deal? What are you talking about?"

He smiled and said, "Do we have a deal?"

I shook his hand and was hooked. Two gimpy knees were already starting to heal as I shifted my focus on how I could get in the best shape possible within the allotted time frame.

A few weeks later, after Barney and Larry decided they wanted to retire from coaching because of their family and work obligations, they introduced me to Dan Jones and Mike Beining, who had both been high school state champions and outstanding Marquette wrestlers.

I expressed my disappointment and surprise at their decision to retire on our way to meet the two new coaches. Larry told me in no uncertain terms, "Freddy, you aren't losing any coaches. We're still going to work on your head. These guys will be able to work on you physically, giving you a good beating every day, to get you in the best shape of your life. Now you have four coaches."

That was the beginning of my college comeback. Over the next two years, I placed in the national tournament as All American with 110 wins and 9 losses and was able to earn the highest finish of any Marquette wrestler ever in the NCAA tournament.

I'm very thankful for my coaches—certainly more than four—and twenty-some training partners, whom my coach Dan Jones recruited to work me as hard as possible to compensate for not having some of the most skilled training partners to work out with.

I also learned that there is a certain level of fitness and excellence one can achieve in which you can beat 90 percent of the competition. Beating the other ten percent, at the skill level I had at that time in my life, seemed depend on other factors, including a little luck.

In all the matches I won when placed in a national tournament, I came from behind in the final minute to win the match, providing more proof that my coaches had prepared me by making sure I had exceptional endurance. Fatigue was never a factor in a match. I could go all out from the first handshake to the second handshake. It's an absolutely different way to compete when you know you won't get tired. Because of my high level of conditioning, I had more patience and confidence that allowed me to create a win before the final buzzer sounded, even though things could go wrong early in the match.

Without Barney, Larry, Dan Jones, Mike Beining, Bob Healy, Frank Galka, and the many others I've mentioned, there would have been no All American honors. I dread to think about how my path might have unfolded as the successes I experienced were instrumental in overcoming hundreds of future challenges over the next thirty years and counting.

* * * *

In 1983, I had two more knee surgeries with Dr. Jim Langenkamp. One day, I was sitting in the hospital and the nurse told me that my knees would never be the same.

My reply, "Nope, they'll be better." I decided during that conversation that I would work on my therapy much longer than the prescribed time to ensure that my knees would be as strong as possible.

When I mentioned this to Dr. Langenkamp, who had been Al McGuire's first recruit when he became head coach at Marquette basketball, Jim mentioned to me that I could run with him on Friday afternoons. Just about every Friday from March through late October that year, we would meet at the North Avenue hill below Milwaukee's famous landmark water tower and do ten sprints up the hill and jog back to the bottom.

I was 28 then and Langenkamp was 37. At 6 foot 6 inches and 230 pounds, he would beat me eight of ten times.

What impressed me about Jim was his commitment, work ethic, and willingness to help me get better and literally back on my feet. Long after that summer, I would train on the North Avenue hill. From Lake Michigan to the water tower was .15 miles from the sewer cover at the bottom of the hill to the end of the railing at the top.

Jim would call me on Friday afternoon to let me know when he was done, then say "OK, Freddy, I'll see you at 4:30 for another edition of the Real Hill Street Blues." (At that time, there was a TV show known as the *Hill Street Blues.)* Our run was always an intense workout. If you're involved in any sport that requires conditioning, I'd recommend you find a hill. Run up and down seven to ten times, sprint for 60 to 90 seconds, and rest for 24 minutes. Repeat until you reach your goal of ten times once a week. This regimen works wonders!

Watertower Hill in Milwaukee-- a tough training ground.

TALENT IS OK, BUT WITHOUT A GOOD WORK ETHIC, IT CAN BE A CURSE

I once coached a kid who was a two-time high school state champion. He would often joke with me that he was a natural. He was good, no doubt about it.

The guy won most of his matches in college. In the big matches, however, somehow his knee would act up. This never happened in the first period; it was always in the middle of the match. It never acted up when he was leading, only when he was behind. Since I was a go-getter coach and less sensitive to him as an athlete because we had competed as teammates, I often referred to his knee as an oxygen tank. When his knee would get sore, the referee would stop the match, which would allow him to catch his breath and have a brief rest.

I'll never know how good he could have been because he was blessed with more talent than most wrestlers ever dreamed of. He did not have to work hard because things came too easy. Therefore, he did not, at that time in his life, have a great work ethic to apply to the sport.

Despite his "bad knee," and as good as this guy was, he was always kind to the people he trained with. In the training room, as a freshman, he could hammer on the seniors, but was always polite and respectful.

Since college, he's been incredibly successful in his business. It's obvious he has worked hard, perhaps learning at deeper level what it takes to win in other aspects of life, which really is the true mark of a champion.

* * * *

CONFIDENCE AND ARROGANCE

Arrogance says: "I'm good and you're nothing." Confidence says: "I'm good and I'm good and I'm good," with little focus on the other person—just on one's ability. It's not something you announce verbally, but it's something you act out literally.

FIRST WIN THE MATCH, THEN PLEASE THE CROWD

Bob Sweet was one year ahead of me at Thomas More and I consider him one of my early mentors. Most people would agree that he was not a flashy wrestler. In fact, some might say his matches were kind of boring. But he would nevertheless win most of the time.

Being new to wrestling, I once asked him why he did not initiate more moves in matches and he said, "If I can counter a move and score, it is all points to me."

I said, "But Bob, if you can chase after some of these guys, you can really make your matches more exciting and have bigger wins."

"Well, Fred, it seems like you haven't heard the pearl of wisdom that advises to first win the match and then please the crowd. There is a lot to be said for those who slow down a match and work hard to be on the right side of the score. I know my style does not thrill the crowd, but my goal is to win matches."

I always remembered that lesson because there is a time for all of us when we want to bust a match wide open. I have noticed that this happens when we are up against an easy opponent. It is really important to compete the same way all the time so that your habits (hopefully good ones) can carry you to success.

Even though Bob Sweet did not compete in college, he was a source of inspiration to me for many years after high school and remains a good friend. As a wrestler, he was a two-time state champion. He usually won the match and ultimately pleased the crowd with his successful results. He is also an inductee of the St. Thomas More Athletic Hall of Fame.

Bob Sweet , state champion in 1972 and 1973.

FIFTEEN YEARS

Throughout the fifteen years I spent in the wrestling room at Marquette, then from after college until I quit wrestling, I do not remember ever being taken down or being scored against. You may think that my memory is gone and I just don't remember, but I could go through many, many workouts and not give up any points.

One advantage I had, being a big fish in a small pond, is that no big fish ever came to my little pond. I could never say that—the small pond of Marquette wrestling compared to the big pond of international competition when I would go to Edinboro, Pennsylvania with Bruce Baumgartner, or to Ohio State with Mark Coleman or Russ Hellickson, or to Stanford with Dan Chaid. They were the big fish in the big pond of world-class competition. It was hard to find training partners in my small pond.

The insight I received was that as I would go to work out at Marquette in my college wrestling room, I would remember the seventeen days and then look back and think about how many years it was since I had been scored on. No matter where you are, in the seventeen days or the fifteen years, those days or years are not who you are, each is just another of the experiences on your path.

Several years later, I was explaining the story of seventeen days to one of my wrestlers. I've coached wrestling for over thirty years, ever since I was in high school. Even when

I was in college, I was coaching high school kids. I was able to master many moves. To me, the word "master" meant that I could wrestle with people at the world-class level and score on them, not just once, but consistently. It's entertaining to think back to all my high school workouts, where kids were flopping around a lot, scoring a lot of points and we thought we were really wrestling well.

Fast-forward twenty-four years, when I was in my last year of competition at age 40. I remember working out with a friend named Dan Chaid. We would work out for an hour or hour and a half, have puddles of sweat around the room because we had the room to ourselves and were able to move around, and we maybe scored 10 points during the whole workout combined. The better we got, the better we were able to counter the moves of others. Many times, in a workout, like in a match, like in life, it's that few seconds or few minutes that can have long-lasting impact on your life. This leads me to believe that it is more about quality than quantity. However, it took a lot of quantity to get me to the quality.

"Hang in there" is the lesson.

SOMETIMES YOUR OPPONENT CAN BE THE BEST PART OF YOUR TEAM

In 1973, as a junior and first-year wrestler at Marquette, I wrestled a guy from St. Catherine's High School in Racine in the finals of the Region 3 Tournament. I lost the match to my opponent, Doug Andrewski, who went on to win the regional title and the following week, won the state title.

For several years, my wrestling buddies called him "The Spoiler" in conversations, because he beat the kid from Pius XI High School. Had Doug lost that match, Pius would have won the tournament. He spoiled Pius' chances of winning the state title, which went to Pacelli High School in Stevens Point, Wisconsin.

Doug would wrestle any opponent, usually volunteering to wrestle All-Americans in higher weight classes to test their abilities. As a junior, he wrestled and won in the 158-, 167-, 177-, 190-pound, and heavyweight classes, even though he never weighed more than 172 pounds himself. He is the only wrestler in the school's history to win in five weight classes, all in one year, including matches against nationally ranked or returning All-American opponents.

After finishing his wrestling career, he got into body-building and was extremely successful in that sport. We also had some mutual friends over the years. Although Doug and

I never really socialized, we had an ongoing, unstated mutual respect for each other.

In 1994, when I was just beginning to train for the Olympics, I was in the Wisconsin Dells, 120 miles from Milwaukee, and ran into Doug and his wife at a restaurant. Initially, we made small talk. "How are you doing? What are you doing these days? Where are you living?"

It turned out that he was living in Racine and I was living in Cudahy, which meant we lived 15 miles from one another. I asked if he was still into weight training; Doug still trained often. I shared with him that over the years I had never really lifted weights that often.

"How did you develop such a large chest if you weren't doing bench presses?" he asked me.

"Every other day, I do a set of pushups, hands on the floor, feet on the chair, as many as I can, until failure. I can usually get to 100 or 120. My personal record is 138. My push-ups aren't just head nods; they're all the way up and all the way down."

I asked him if I could get some pointers to make sure I was training properly and he said, "Well, you can just train with me."

For the next two and a half years, integrated into my schedule was training with Doug and one of his workout partners, Sam. Sam was not as big as we were, so when it came to the heavy lifts, he would often have to bow out, but one thing Sam taught me was the value of consistent, disciplined workouts. Sam was there every day we were scheduled and I learned from Sam the importance of being ready. I was totally confident in my strength because I was able to bench press 525 pounds and do a leg press in a hip sled of 2,010 pounds eleven times. I understand that moving 2,010 pounds eleven times is hard to comprehend, but I had plenty of witnesses who saw me do this and a couple of them were there to pull me out from under the machine when my legs were completely "smoked," when your muscles are so full of lactic acid that you can't do any more.

Because of my strength training, I had total confidence in my durability. I knew that if I were bounced around on the mat, I just had to dust myself off and get back into the fight. I attribute Doug's commitment and mentorship as the single most valuable aspect of my training during my last attempt to make the U.S. Olympic Freestyle Wrestling Team. When I started training with Doug, I certainly was already strong, but not in the specialized areas that he taught me and helped me develop so well.

When I was a kid, there was a TV show called *The 6-Million Dollar Man,* which was about a human with bionic, mechanical limbs. *The Bionic Woman* was another TV show airing at the same time. When we worked out and I would break through a new personal record on a certain lift, Doug would often shake his head and say, "So much for bionics. This guy's hydraulic." When I competed, Doug would often be on "my chair," next to one of "my dads," Larry O'Neil, watching the match with total confidence that I would not get hurt or be overpowered.

Remember, Doug had been my opponent in high school. It takes a bit of maturity to let go of your ego and reach out to others, just as it takes some common sense to make sure that as your team grows, you include those who can help you be your best. For me, Doug was that person.

Doug's wife, Jeanne, was a very successful bodybuilder, and it was her input and guidance that kept me on track with the nutritional aspects of my training. With her help, I was able to recover from my intense workouts much faster by using supplements.

People asked me from time to time if I ever used steroids. I often joked that the only steroids I ever took were pasta and pizza. I am thankful that even though I occasionally saw others using steroids in all kinds of sports, I never felt the need or had the desire to go down that path. I attribute such wise decisions to the mentors and friends who were the strongest influences in my life.

Even though I enjoyed having a beer once in a while, I practiced a principle from my college days in economics class called the "Law of Diminishing Returns." Put into a real-life situation, it means that when you have something like an ice cream cone, or some other treat, it's the first one that tastes the best. As you have more, there is a diminishing return in terms of your sense of satisfaction. Even though I enjoyed having pasta and pizza, I noticed that one or two servings were the optimal amount. Any more than that would severely affect my ability to train the next day.

Over the years, it has become obvious to me that I picked the wrong sport to try to exemplify the saying "The only thing you should take in extreme is moderation." In the sport of wrestling, you have to train yourself in such a way that you can go all out for extended periods of time so that you have no attention on your breathing or lung capacity and can focus on the techniques you have developed and fine-tuned.

Jeannie Andrewski

Doug and Jeannie Andrewski, bodybuilding champions, with family.

SASKIA AND JOS

Saskia and Jos are my dearest friends. This wonderful couple happens to live in Amsterdam in the Netherlands. I met them back in 1996 when I was training for the Olympic Trials.

Jos (pronounced "yos") is a master at Weng Chun. Weng Chun is a Chinese martial art similar to Kung Fu. The name, literally translated, means "eternal power of life" or "everlasting springtime."

Jos is, no doubt, one of the toughest men I've ever met and he's never wrestled a day in his life. Saskia is one of the most beautiful women you could ever meet. However, it's their intelligence and their kindness that are their dominant traits. They have no ego about their looks or their strength. In February, 2010, they surprised me with a phone call to tell me that they had named their new baby girl "Frederique" after me.

I was introduced to Jos through a mutual friend of ours as I was looking for a way to integrate new mental skills and deeper meditation techniques to enhance my training. In January of 1996, I got his phone number and called him. We talked for about an hour. I explained my goals to him and we both shared about our backgrounds. Over the next several weeks, we talked several times, and in April that same year, Jos and Saskia came to the US to visit me and help me train on the mental aspects of the sport.

They were instrumental in me going deeper on a personal level to let go of various limiting beliefs that I possessed, but was not totally conscious of. They were extremely helpful in the birth of my new path, which would evolve after my Olympic training program was over, of personal growth like never before. Although I do not consider myself religious, I must share with you that I have an incredibly strong faith. The labels that people use for a higher power or even a denomination, although very important to them, are not as important to me as knowing how my spirituality and reality can coexist and complement each other.

At that time, I was always working on selling life insurance, had my embroidery company with about sixty employees, and was very busy in my head—so busy that I was never really anywhere, because I was thinking of where I just was, where I had to be next, or what I had to do instead of being in the present moment. It was obvious to me at that time that I had to focus on relaxing. Try to do it some time. You just have to relax—you can't focus on it.

I learned a lot of things from Saskia and Jos that could be books on their own. More than anything, they taught me is that if you want to really grow, focus less on grasping things and more on letting go because letting go frees you up on deeper levels. It seems congruent with the proverb, "It's not what you have, but what has you."

I would reflect on getting clearer about what I wanted in my life and also what I didn't want. By doing an inventory on your life, you will find a lot of things that don't serve you or aren't helpful any more. You may also discover that your lifetime goal has changed as you let go of old beliefs.

A life inventory is simply a written review of key experiences you have had and are having, goals you've set in the past and may or may not have achieved, goals you now have for the future, and an assessment of whether or not past experiences, attitudes, and goals serve your future plans. Once you establish where you've been and define clearly where you want to go, you have just completed the first step to experiencing the life you desire and so much deserve.

I have heard lots of preachers, leaders, and others talk about love at an intellectual level, but love cannot be communicated in the mind alone. It must be experienced, not just thought about. Jos and Saskia don't talk about love; they live it. They are two of the most loving people I've ever met. They are this way with everyone they meet. I remember hearing that love draws, it doesn't demand. There is something about Jos and Saskia that has drawn many people to them from all kinds of circles.

Nor do Jos and Saskia seem bound by the traditional hustle and bustle of the rest of the world. No matter whom they're talking to or what they're doing, they're always present to that activity with their full attention. When they interact with you, you can sense a deep kind of love that flows through them back to you.

Fred, Russ, Saskia Jos (1996)

In February, 2010, Jos and Saskia had a
daughter, whom they named Frederique.

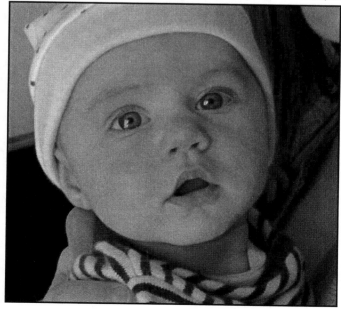

WHAT WOULD YOU DO
IF YOU KNEW YOU
COULDN'T FAIL?

In March, 1994, I was introduced to a woman who was a life coach, at that time a new industry. She worked with people to help them fine-tune the weaker aspects of their lives to convert those into strengths, so they would experience personal growth. In our conversation, we concluded that I didn't really seem to be willing to be coached or see the need for it. We met just a few more times over the next month or so.

During one of our discussions, she asked, "What would you do if you knew you couldn't fail?"

In less than one second, I said, "I would train for the Olympic team to win a gold medal in wrestling."

Her name was Kristin. She was surprised at my answer, even though I wasn't. Then, she asked, "What would you say when you walk off the mat after a match, dripping sweat and huffing and puffing, making a mess?"

I said I needed a minute. I was quiet for about a minute and then had the answer. I would say, "This is a strange sport. Other than wrestling, judo and boxing are the only sports in which you have to physically beat someone to excel and win a medal. In track, rowing, and gymnastics, you have to do your best to come in first. In your life, if you are getting beat up, get help, and protection so that doesn't have to happen anymore. If you're beating someone up, stop doing it and understand that if you really want to be tough and show strength, learn to be gentle. There is nothing stronger than gentleness and there is nothing more gentle than strength. Then I would walk away from the microphone. It would be a platform for me to begin speaking publicly about the problems with domestic abuse."

I WOULD USE THE MEDAL AS A PLATFORM
TO SAY THAT TOUGH GUYS CAN BE GENTLE.

That conversation was the impetus for me to decide, in one moment, that I would commit the next two and a half years of my life to training for the Olympics. I got together with my former wrestling coaches, Dan Jones, Frank Galka, two of my adopted brothers, and Barney Karpfinger, Larry O'Neil, Russ Hellickson, Andy Rein, Brian Weber, Tom Burns, and a former opponent of mine, Doug Andrewski.

I put my team together and got to work. I also contacted Russ Hellickson, who was the coach at Ohio State University, who then contacted Bruce Baumgartner. Bruce was the defending Olympic champion and someone I had trained with before. Russ was instrumental in getting me to work out with his own wrestling club at Ohio State. I would work out with Bruce periodically when I would go to Edinboro, Pennsylvania, for five-day stretches. Bruce was the head wrestling coach of the University of Pennsylvania– Edinboro's wrestling team and now serves as the athletic director.

It was amazing to me how everything started to fall in place once I made the decision. My strength guy showed up. My technique guy showed up. I already had a great work ethic for conditioning. Things were moving right along. Over the next two years, things went along smoothly with minimal injuries—twists and sprains, but nothing severe—lots of trips to the Olympic training center, Edinboro, Columbus, Ohio, and Stanford to train with several of the best wrestlers in the world.

The old proverb says, "As iron sharpens iron, so one person sharpens another," is no more true than in our sport. When you tell people who you work out with, they know your level of ability and likelihood of success. I can honestly say that I got to train with the best in the world on a consistent basis.

Other than the two weeks during which I grieved the Dave Schultz tragedy, when Dave, a 1984 Olympic champion who was training for the 1996 games, was shot and killed in 1996, I never took more than one day off in any given week.

*   *   *   *

Anyway, I was cruising along in training and wrestling really well until I got to the US Open. I wrestled Bruce Baumgartner and got pounded in that match. We'd been working out together for many months and I could offer a million excuses, but they won't change the outcome, so I'll leave it that I got beat up.

After the match, I went back to my hotel room with Jos and Saskia and discussed what had happened. For the next three hours, I sobbed like a little boy. Ironically, but not unexpectedly, little boy stuff came up about things I was willing to talk about, but not publish. I'm complete with it in my life, but do not feel the need to retaliate and open a Pandora's box to punish those who harmed me when I was very vulnerable. I have since decided, many times, to forgive the whole thing and have, myself, come to a place of love for these people because out of these experiences, I have developed incredibly positive aspects of my life in spite of the negative impact of their behaviors.

When I was crying, one of the biggest things I noticed was that I thought I wasn't going to get to tell my story about strength and gentleness because I had lost my opportunity to be on the platform. If I lost by a point or two, I'd still be in the running, but getting blown out was too much to overcome and if I was thirty, it would have been much different from when I was forty, because I got everything I could out of my body that would allow me to compete on that level. I had a limiting belief that I had to do it a certain way. That certain way was to win a gold medal, which would give me credibility to speak. I then created this path of sadness and I became tired, physically exhausted, because I over-trained.

A few weeks later, I competed in the final trials. I was able to qualify for the final trials through three different tournaments. Because I was not the champion of the US Open, I had to work my way up the ladder. In the last match I wrestled, I lost 1-0. I was proud that I played nice, even though it was a controlled fight, and that I always took the high road in competition. I never used cheap shots or compromised doing what was right when trying to win. It was very clear to me that I didn't have to do this any more. As far as my wrestling chapter, I was complete.

Later events revealed to me that the extent of my expression of sadness after I lost that match in the US Open was directly related to the importance I placed on the significance of needing to have a gold medal to talk about the issue of domestic abuse issue. It also revealed an aspect of my own self of wanting to make a difference in a big, measurable way, only to find out later that we all make a difference whether we want to or not. Based simply on the fact that we're here, we make a difference. The degree of difference is always contingent upon our commitment, but we do make a difference.

Perhaps you, too, may want to fine tune and define in detail how you could improve your life by making a positive difference in the lives of others. Remember, we all get what we give.

TRAINING FOR
THE OLYMPICS

I was thirty-eight years old and decided to start training for the 1996 Olympic team, which would put me at forty years old during the Olympic trials and competition. On one occasion, about a year and a half into my training, maybe two months before the U.S. Open and very close to my fortieth birthday, I was wrestling at the University of Pennsylvania—Edinboro with Bruce Baumgartner and Rulon Gardner. One day, I wrestled three matches with each guy. I wrestled Bruce for three matches and Rulon for three matches. I won two of three matches with each guy. The second day, I won one out of three with each guy. The third day, I won zero out of three with Bruce and one out of three with Rulon.

We would usually train for five days at a time, having intense wrestling workouts on one day and then lifting or conditioning on our alternate workout days. Having the opportunity to train with these guys was an honor. Again, more good people. Bruce Baumgartner has won more Olympic medals than any American Olympic wrestler ever. Rulon Gardner, although I trained with him in 1996, went on to win a gold medal in 2000, defeating Alexander Karelin of Russia. Gardner's defeat of Karelin to win the gold medal was the upset of the tournament because Karelin had won the previous three Olympics in that weight class. In 2004, Rulon continued to compete and won a bronze medal, again proving that ability coupled with persistence can lead to a world-class performance. Those who trained with Rulon would agree that his work ethic and conditioning were exceptional. It was no surprise to any of us that he became an Olympic champion.xxx

The reason I reflect back to when I was forty years old was because it was just a couple of years later that my father had a series of strokes that left him confined to a wheelchair. About that time, I remember seeing a story on one of the network TV magazines, like *20/20, 60 Minutes, Dateline*—I don't recall which one it was. There was a guy on the show who was a world-class athlete and somehow ended up in a wheelchair. There was a quote in the story where he responded to a question about what the hardest thing was for him now that he was confined to the wheelchair. He said, "I miss doing all the things I used to hate to do." I was very thankful to be able to compete at the Olympic level at forty years old. I was incredibly thankful that my body was durable and that I had training partners who were great athletes and really nice people.

Along the way, I also had the opportunity to train with Olympian Mark Coleman, 1984 Olympic Champion Lou Banach, world-class wrestler Dan Chaid, 1960 Olympic Champion Doug Blubaugh, Laurent Soucie, Mitch Hull, and had a lot of help and guidance from friends like Andy Rein and Dave Schultz. Doug Blubaugh was a 1960 Olympic champion and MVP of the tournament. Laurent Soucie was a

1975 NCAA Division 1 All American and two-times USA Senior Freestyle Champion. Mark Coleman was a 1992 Olympian at 220 pounds. Dan Chaid was a four-time NCAA Division I All American and won the NCAA Division I Championship in 1984-85. Mitch Hull was an Olympic alternate in 1984 and Champion of the Pan Am Games.

These are just a few of the many people I worked with on my path to be my best. Even though I have no Olympic or World hardware to show you because I never won one of the coveted medals, I have, through my work ethic and strong desire to improve, been able to win the respect of these people and enjoy their friendship. The old proverb is, "As iron sharpens iron, so one man sharpens another."

IF YOU'RE OPEN-MINDED, YOU CAN LEARN FROM ANYONE

One day in 1996, I was in the Olympic wrestling room in Colorado Springs, Colorado. I had just completed a workout with the other Olympic team members. Ten high school wrestlers were waiting on the sidelines, getting ready to use the mats.

I was completely out of steam from my workout and just needed to cool down. While the others left, I took my time and started to watch the kids as they were showing each other how to flip an opponent onto his back. One kid was an up-and-coming junior at an area high school in Colorado Springs. I was watching them discuss the movement and after about ten minutes of just observing them from the side, I asked if I could ask a question. Whenever I wrestled, I would bring several shirts with me, because after working out for about fifteen minutes, I would be completely drenched. Now I put on a fresh shirt and was cooled off.

I asked the boy from Colorado Springs if he would demonstrate the move on me because I wanted to feel where the pressure was coming from. I weighed more than 280 pounds and he was about 170 pounds, an obvious mismatch in size. I was amazed, when I lay on the mat and he stepped on top and tried to flip me over, once he applied certain parts of the move to me, I couldn't recover. For the next twenty minutes, we continued to discuss the move and he showed it to me in great detail.

I then practiced the move on a guy who was about 220 pounds. The high school student looked on and I fine-tuned the move so I could have the three triggers to complete the move. It was called "step, load, and lift." When I stepped, I would scoop up the guy's far arm and lift him off the mat. Once that was done, my opponent could not recover to get back to his base, and he was on his back fighting for his life.

Over the next two months, I drilled that move every day for at least fifty repetitions. Then I got to the U.S. Open for the Olympics. My first three matches were all tight matches with scores of 0-0 or I was winning by one or two points. In each of those matches, my opponent was lax for a couple of seconds, which allowed me to step in, load, and lift. I pinned my first three opponents in the U.S. Open at age forty in bouts against guys in their mid-twenties using a move I learned from a sixteen-year-old eight weeks earlier. (In fact, the shorts I was wearing when he showed me the move said "Marquette Wrestling." I had gotten them when I was in school at Marquette in 1979, so the shorts were older than he was!)

Keep an open mind; you can learn from anyone. We should all remember that what's important in life is not knowing things, but rather, applying what we know. It seems a pity that we all know the things we need to do, but seldom apply that knowledge.

JUDGMENT

You may have heard the comment that you will be judged by the same measure you use to judge others. A preacher usually tells you this. As I developed my interpretation of judgment, I came to a different conclusion for a different reason.

I learned in wrestling that if I focused on my opponent—perhaps noticing the fact that he was bulging with muscles or bulging with pudginess, simply had a skinny build, or whatever—my judgment was always wrong. Guys who were pudgy, but with incredible quickness, would convince me that they weren't that pudgy after all because they would beat me. Conversely, I wrestled guys who were muscle magazine material and would run out of gas and just quit as I pinned them.

Over the years, I learned that whenever I judged someone and didn't notice I was judging that person, I was held hostage by the judgment.

Let me go deeper. When you judge someone, it fixes your attention on that label. Only when that label is destroyed can you let go of your judgment. The pudgy wrestler with incredible speed would convince me that my label was wrong and the muscular wrestler with no endurance would convince me that my label was wrong. I let go of my labels.

Even though I may meet someone about whom I might have judgment, I notice the judgment and wonder what the person is really like. It is possible to meet someone and say,

"There is a smart person and I wonder what he or she's really like, or tough, warm, smart, pretty, handsome, cold, and so on, always completing the sentence with, 'I wonder what he or she's really like.'" That allows me to notice my judgment without judging myself and just let it go by as a simple observation.

The more quickly you let go of your judgments, the more instantaneously you will be able to intuitively comprehend what people really are about.

If you judge someone, your judgment will prove you wrong every time. Don't judge others, because you will miss a lot.

FOCUS

I learned from my own experience as an athlete and reinforced the belief over the next more than thirty years that coaching doesn't only occur during matches; it goes on between the matches as well. The trips to and from events are usually the best opportunity for coaching because you're riding in a car or van and you're talking about different things and somehow your sport comes up.

Coaching between matches happens often. During the match, the coach may share points of fine-tuning to get an athlete through the next phase of the competition. The best coaches I have run across are big-picture people who are also able to focus on any detail at the same time, so they're able to coach the wrestler on the details during the match and look at the big picture outside the match.

A lot of problems don't happen the day they occur— they actually take place long before they manifest. For example, every day people get married and divorced. If you ask any of them when they got married, they'll give you a date. They'll also tell you the date of their divorce. If you dig deeper and ask about things like when the relationships began to change, either being drawn together or beginning to drift apart, they can often describe the incidents that were turning points.

IF YOU DON'T REACT, YOU ARE ALWAYS POWERFUL

Halfway through my training for the 1996 Olympics, in 1995, I attended a two-week martial arts seminar in Oakland, California. The people who attended the seminars were all 3rd-degree black belts or higher in their respective sports and were considered masters in their style of martial arts. When applying to attend this event, I had to complete a resume that included the times I placed high in the national tournaments and explain my years of coaching and training before I was allowed to attend the seminar.

One time, we were about to start a session and I had a training partner, who at 170 pounds, was one hundred pounds lighter than me. We worked on some of the techniques together. When the training session started, he mentioned he wanted to work with me more because he trained with a lot of bigger men and wanted to be sure his techniques would be effective on a big guy.

Just before the class started, as my training partner was standing there relaxed, I stepped up to him, grabbed his right wrist with my right hand and his right elbow with my left hand, and pulled it to my chest. I was very slowly moving his arm around assessing the moves available to me. He said to me, in a really calm voice, as he looked me right in the eyes, "Fred, if you really think about it, you don't want that arm."

That's all he said. I felt such a wave of confidence and kindness that I immediately let go of the arm, stepped back and asked why I wouldn't want the arm. He answered, "Because you get everything that comes with it, and you don't want my arm."

When I grabbed his wrist, he had no reaction. Later in the seminar, I asked him why. He said that in his life, when he has no tenseness in his arm, he's able to move faster because he didn't need to stop the tenseness before he began his move. It gave him the freedom to do what he needed to do when he needed to do it. It was a great moment of teaching for me to learn the power of not reacting.

Let's go back in time to the mid-1980s. I was invited to wrestle at the University of Wisconsin–Madison wrestling room when one of the Asian national teams was hosted by Wisconsin for a few days as they were traveling around the country. I received a call from Russ Hellickson around 10:00 a.m. and he said the teams would be working out that afternoon and that I would be welcome to come.

In those days, I was a full-time insurance agent and I remember getting to Madison, taking off my suit, and putting on my wrestling outfit. It definitely was a changing of identities because the work as an agent for a major insurance company is verbal and mental, and I was going to be wrestling with other world-class athletes, so I had to engage mentally and physically.

I didn't take the time to warm up properly—no running and only minimal stretching—and we began to wrestle. My partner was a member of his national wrestling team. For the first five minutes of our workout, I got thrown around like a rag doll. Getting warmed up is not a big deal if two rookie wrestlers are just going to roll around on the mat, but I was working out with a world-class wrestler at an intense pace.

Generally, I never get thrown. After getting launched into the wall, I decided I'd better get warmed up before I got seriously hurt. I went over to the bilingual coach and explained to him that I needed a few minutes to "rinse out," which translates as "get water to get warmed up more."

I went to the restroom, returned, and began running. I was much more warmed up and decided to lower my stance, focus more on my breathing, and said an affirmation, "I score, I score," so my focus shifted. For the next forty-five minutes, I pounded on this guy. He might have scored on me five more times in the next fifty exchanges.

After we were all done wrestling, the bilingual coach asked me if I wanted to ask the other wrestler any questions. Apparently, he asked the same of the other wrestler. I nodded. For the Korean wrestler, the coach asked, "How did you get so fast? For a big man, I am amazed at how fast you are."

I told him I learned to drill moves by practicing thousands of times, as well as by teaching others. My question to my partner was, "How come, when you were taking me down in the first few minutes and we were wrestling in the last fifty minutes, you always had the same neutral expression on your face?"

He smiled as the coach translated this to him. After the words came back, the coach said, "When he was a little boy, before he was five years old, his grandfather was a master martial arts teacher. His parents would take him to the school where his grandfather taught many students. His grandfather would allow him to participate in the class, but he had to complete the whole class—each session he started—or he had to sit in a chair while the class was on and watch. After sitting in the chair for a few days, he learned it was easier to get involved. His grandfather taught him many lessons that he uses in wrestling. The one you're speaking of is, no matter what happens, if you don't react, even though you might not be winning, you are still in your own power. His grandfather taught him, "When you don't react, you're always powerful."

*   *   *   *

Think of the last time you were upset about something, whether it was traffic, a line, being on hold—so what. If you start to say "It will all work out," like Larry told me thousands of times, that affirmation will begin the process of things all working out.

People react with anger, frustration, and sarcasm. Whenever you react with emotions, you are weakened. Those feelings cause you to lose your focus and prevent you from experiencing the intended or desired outcome. When you react in a negative way, you just got scored on. Don't get scored on!

SLOW IS FAST

I remember reading an ancient Chinese proverb, "Slow is fast." This simply means that sometimes the fastest way to get things done is step by step, which may seem slow, but is ultimately the fastest way.

I often teach "slow is fast" when I coach wrestling. I do a move called an arm drag. In this move, you touch my shoulder, I lean into you so that you have to lean more into me, and then I swing my arms around, hooking your arm, so I am able to pull you past me and step around you. I know it's complicated to try to communicate a wrestling move in words, but I've done the arm drag at least a couple of hundred thousand times because I have taught easily a couple of thousand kids that move one-on-one since I learned the move myself over 39 years ago.

When I show the move to the youngsters, even though I'm in my fifties, I still notice that it is very fluid and they notice it, too. Sometimes I'll hear an "Ooh, wow, he's fast," but when you practice a move a couple of hundred thousand times, you get fast.

When I was in my thirties, I competed in different tournaments. In one tournament, I wrestled a match where I took a guy down eleven times with an arm drag. As I walked off the mat, the guy said, "You're really a natural."

I responded, "When you do a move 100,000 times, you're a natural." I smiled. The guy smiled and a few seconds later, a high school senior came up and sat next to him in the stands. I remember telling the youngster that if he wanted to learn more about that move, I'd be happy to share it with him. Before the tournament was over, we spent about twenty minutes working on the arm drag. The first thing I told him was that if you want to learn the move fast, do it slow, because slow is fast.

How many times in our lives do we want to learn the "good stuff" or the interesting stuff fast from a technical seminar, class, or when learning a simple meditation? Remember that "slow is fast." It is only when you take in all of the information that you can truly understand the "good stuff."

Again, there are no shortcuts. You can take shortcuts, but expect the consequences of that decision.

NO LIGHT

In 1995, I was coaching at a high school where my nephew, Timmy (my sister Christine's son) was on the wrestling team. He competed in the conference tournament and wound up losing the first round in a tight match, 1-0, to a guy he had beaten before. For me, it was a frustrating match to watch because the opponent kept doing the same move, tying up my nephew's ankle. They were so well matched in ability that there would be enough activity to justify the official not calling either one for stalling. As the seconds ticked down, the buzzer sounded, and Timmy lost the match.

The guy Timmy lost to went on to lose his next round, so now Timmy was out of the tournament. He was the team captain, the previous year Wisconsin state runner-up, and he didn't get to wrestle any more in that tournament. In those days, our program was so stacked with talent that we could always afford to lose one or two of our best guys and still win by a healthy margin. This was the case that year.

After the tournament was over, I ended up going out with a co-coach of mine named Scott Grudzinski, and a couple of coaches from another school, Brian Weber and Rob Morales. We started talking about our high school records; all of us had been top wrestlers back then.

In high school, Scott's record had been 108-11. He had been amazing to watch because he was so fast that at 112 pounds, he would push on his opponent as they both stood on their feet, and the next second, the other guy was on his back. It was that quick. Scott was instrumental in the program I was coaching at the time because of his attention to detail in teaching techniques, sequences, and the finer aspects of each move. I began calling Scott "The Doctor" because of his gift for communicating fine teaching details.

It was after that conversation that Scott started calling me "The Professor," because he noticed that I would often come up with insights on situations we were experiencing that were more long-term and philosophical in nature. To this day, whenever Scott and I talk, it's always, "How's the Doctor?" and he'll say, "How's the Professor?" This is just another example of the respect for our fellow wrestlers bred by our sport.

Back to the dinner. Brian Weber was one of the first state champions I ever coached. Brian's high school record was 81-10 and he was no doubt one of the best wrestlers out of our high school. Brian continued to wrestle in college at Long Beach State and then transferred to the University of Wisconsin-Madison, from which he graduated. He was a great competitor and a thorough technician. Rob Morales, a "hammer" (meaning he was very tough), was also a state champion a year after Brian was.

The four of us began talking about how our teams had performed that day. The team I was coaching won the conference championship. Morales' and Weber's team took third that day.

Rob expressed his disappointment that his nephew (who was a junior) had not won by more than ten points.

I asked, "Are you for real?"

He said, "Yeah, I'm for real. He should win all matches by superior decisions."

I was thinking that my nephew Timmy, a senior, had just lost 1-0 and didn't get to wrestle the rest of the day because he was out of the tournament. I was thankful Timmy hadn't gotten hurt and knew we would be back and would sort things out the next time he met up with that opponent.

Morales was upset about a point that hadn't even determined the victory of the match. With a smile, I responded, "Wow. That's really intense."

Rob showed me what he meant. "Look at this." He held his hand up in my face, with his index finger pressed tightly against his thumb. Then he asked, "What do you see?"

I said, "Nothing."

He said, "Right. No light."

I said, "No light? What does that mean?"

Rob responded, "When a kid wrestles, he should be so focused that there is no chance of the opponent winning. That's what I call 'no light.' Nothing. No points, no light."

I started laughing and said, "Rob, these are high school kids."

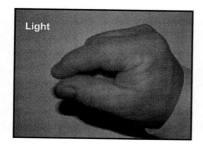

He said, "So what? They can still win big."

Over the next two years, Morales' nephew, Rudy Ruiz, not only didn't get scored on, he won every match. He was a three-time state champion and the most successful high school wrestler ever to come out of St. Thomas More, many years after I graduated from there. Rudy went on to Stanford and excelled on the Division I College level.

Rudy had the opportunity to wrestle a four-time state champ from Wisconsin, Kevin Black, in an NCAA Division I College Wrestling Tournament. Kevin, himself a four-time high school state champion, was an outstanding athlete. He gave Rudy all he could in one of the matches at the national tournament. However, Rudy was able to win the tight match. Two champions wrestled the match, but only one got to win that day.

I couldn't help but think about how the "no light" conversation may have been instrumental in this match, as well. Things never happen when they happen. They happen long before. It seemed to work that way here again. When you look at the match between Kevin Black and Rudy Ruiz, it is yet another example of the great respect for our fellow wrestlers that our sport breeds. Not everyone can win, but there are no losers when people work hard to be their best.

ALL IT TAKES IS ALL YOU GOT AND THEY FLY EVERY TIME

I remember going to Mitchell Field, the Milwaukee airport, on my bicycle with my older brother, Rick, when he was twelve and I was nine. We would take a couple peanut butter and jelly sandwiches and some soda (with a can opener in those days) and declare a day at the airport, which was always over by 3:00 p.m. when our father would be home from work.

We would sit at the end of the runway and watch the planes pull up, line up, and take off. Rick had a big pocket watch. I would count the time it took the planes to take off. I remember the numbers twenty-five and forty-five because It would take small planes about 25 seconds and the larger planes up to 45 seconds to go from a dead stop to being airborne.

When I wrestled, I followed the same philosophy. The planes would line up, go all out, and succeed every time. I would think about being like a jet (a 280-pound jet) and focus on accelerating to beat my previous workout times. When I went all out, I knew what I could do, and that way, no matter what, I would have no regrets. Today, when I look back on how I trained in earlier days, I seldom recall how hard I worked, but I always remember the positive outcomes and I am thankful for all the successes I did enjoy.

In many ways, wrestling is a funny sport. You are the team. You have no place to hide. However, you find out quickly that you need good people surrounding you. You need training partners. You need specialists in every facet of what you are attempting to become. When people asked me, "What makes a wrestler good?" I would always ask back, "When?"

In high school, you can have success based on strength, or conditioning, or technique. One of these qualities can carry you a long way. In college, you can win a lot by having two of these components. However, at the world-class level, everyone is strong, aerobically well conditioned, and has great technique, so it is a much bigger challenge to create a significant difference.

In the final 1996 Olympic trials, three of the ten US Olympians won their matches in overtime, in a sudden victory situation, in their third matches of the best of three. Two of the US team members went on to win Olympic medals, Tom Brands and Kendall Cross.

At those Olympic trials, I was not the top guy. If you are not the top guy and if you are at the Olympics, you are watching, not competing. No matter what I did after all that intensive, disciplined athletic training, I still felt sad after I got back from attending the Olympics as a spectator rather than as a competitor.

As an observer at the Olympic games, I realized that many of the best athletes from other countries would not have been able to place in our U.S. Open, the qualifying tournament for the U.S. Olympic team. They just weren't good enough. The fact that the U.S. training programs are far superior to those of many other countries is a common topic of discussion. If you get to the top ten in any other major professional sport, you are going to be famous.

Not so with wrestling. Having spent time with members of the U.S. Olympic wrestling teams, with guys like Kurt Angle, Ed Banach, Lou Banach, Bruce Baumgartner, Doug Blubaugh, Terry and Tom Brands, Kendall Cross, Melvin Douglas, Steve Fraser, Dan Gable, Rulon Gardner, Matt Ghafarri, Russ Hellickson, Mike Houck, Leroy Kemp, Kenny Monday, Steve Neal, Ben Peterson, John Peterson, Andy Rein, Bill Scherr, Jim Scherr, Mark Schultz, Dave Schultz, and John Smith over the years, I observed that no one has a clue that these guys are all legends of our sport.

Each of these men, for a small window of time, enjoyed the limelight as world or Olympic champion or medalist. Ten of them were my training partners; I was proud to help them improve as I improved my own conditioning, skills, and confidence. "As iron sharpens iron, so does one man sharpen another" is never truer than in the one-on-one sport of wrestling. It is truly a sport of respectful gentlemen.

Future Olympians?
The author in 2007, lifting Billy Mitchell (265 lbs) and Charlie Mitchell (215 lbs) after they won the regional tournament, which put them one step closer to the state championships. I had the opportunity to coach Charlie, Billy, and now Tommy Mitchell. Charlie has the most varsity wins at his high school with 111 victories. Billy held the most wins on record in a single season with 44 victories, and tied the best finish in the history of the school as a state runner-up in 2010.

"GUARD YOUR HEART & GUARD YOUR MIND" SO THAT YOU'LL BE READY

There is a proverb in the Old Testament that says, "Above all, guard your heart." For centuries, people have and will continue to debate the interpretation of all kinds of verses, quips, clichés, adages, and so on.

"Guarding your heart" can be interpreted many ways. If you really guard your heart, you might never fall in love or be vulnerable in any way. My interpretation of "guard your heart" is to guard your mind. This is based on the Hebrew translation of the word "heart," which refers to the mind. If you really guard your mind, you will be very selective in what you allow to enter.

One of the first things I notice people allowing into their minds is music, under the pretext of "psyching themselves up." When I coached, I often saw athletes with earphones, listening to some kind of "motivational" music just before a big match, I would ask what they were listening to, and then listen to it myself.

I would ask them to turn their earphones off and to get running at a slow jog, focusing on their breathing, so that when they started their matches, their bodies were warmed up. Often, I would share with them my belief that getting psyched up for a match (for instance, with aggressive music) is counterproductive because it means approaching a physical fight with emotional preparation.

Although our emotions are very important, in a controlled fight situation, feelings make it difficult to focus on the physical aspects of the match. Getting too wrapped up emotionally can result in your being pounded on or attacked by the physical moves of your opponent.

I would also tell my athletes that getting psyched up was only good until the first thing goes wrong. When that happens, you need to return as quickly as possible to your real situation: the reality of the match or the controlled fight. It was amazing how often the headphones fell away after my explanations.

Before the matches, the kids would run or drill with a partner, getting their bodies warm, so that whenever the whistle blew, they were in the moment and ready. They were guarding their minds.

"Being ready" also meant drilling a move many times. While that may feel boring, on the other side of the routine move is the excitement of being in a big match with a worthy opponent, and having your move so well mastered that the other guy can't stop it. You can then do your move six, eight or ten times in a match and bust the match wide open in an extremely lopsided victory. That can be a lot of fun and is certainly not boring.

You will find in your life, whether it is wrestling, another sport, or another part of life in which you want to excel, if you can break anything down to its smallest details, master each detail individually, and then put them all back together in segments, you will be ready for whatever you are doing.

In wrestling, I feel it's arrogant to go out in a match and try a new move against a very seasoned wrestler when you haven't worked hard enough to master the move. That athlete will usually show you and most likely convince you that it was a nice try, send you packing back home because it did not work, and you'll have to go back to the drawing board because the move was ineffective. I know there are exceptions, but in wrestling and other learned skills, I would rather stick with the higher probability of success gained through perfect practice. By being prepared, you are guarding your mind, and are ready for anything.

My friend Mike Coakley would often say, "It's not practice that makes perfect, but perfect practice that makes perfect."

BE YOURSELF

How many times have we all said, especially when we were growing up, "I wish I were like so and so? He or she has it so easy."

As I've gotten to know many people over the years, people of all walks of life, from different cultures and countries, is that we all have one thing in common.

We are all like the moon. We all have a dark side that many people never get to see. To some, the dark side can be very simple and to others, the dark side can be criminal. Regardless, the dark side is something we're not proud of and don't let out too easily.

How many times have we thought we wanted to be like someone else, only to find out that that person's path wasn't that much fun after all, or that their path appeared to be easy at one point, but then ended up being very difficult.

Being content with your life and focusing on what you are thankful for, regardless of your circumstances, helps give you perspective.

This contentment can enhance your life with richness on many levels. Simply said, wanting to be another person is to waste the person you are.

BEING IN BUSINESS

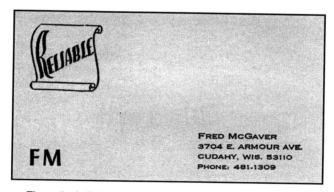

The author's first business card, created when he was eleven.

PAPER BOY

I remember being five years old and riding on the crossbar of my oldest brother's bike when he would take me for a ride. He was fifteen and I was five. He was the paperboy on our street, Armour Avenue. My second oldest brother, Joe, had the street to the north called Van Norman Avenue. I would sometimes ride in the car with my dad and brothers and put the papers at my grade school friends' homes while I learned about the newpaper business and delivering the paper.

It took six more years, when I was eleven, to have my own paper routes, which I continued for the next five years. I had a couple of neighborhood friends help me. I would pay them during the week and then do the whole route myself on Sundays, with my dad or one of my older brothers driving his car for me on the route with the papers in the back. I would run to houses in a four-block area, come back, and get more papers. Because I was afraid of the dark, and it was always dark in the morning, I would run as fast as I could. (Later, when I went out for sports in high school, that weekly, three-hour endurance training session made a big difference in my aerobic conditioning).

Over the years, my paper route customer list grew to over 100 people. I got to know just about all of them. Several were retired people who had lived in Cudahy all their lives. They would often tell me stories about what Cudahy was like when they were young. It was very interesting to hear stories about the 1920s and 1930s, when the full city blocks only had two or three houses on each. While talking to these folks, I began to realize that change occurred regardless—for every age, for every person—and that to expect or want things not to change is unrealistic, probably unhealthy, and for sure unlikely.

I used to give to all the customers on my paper route my business card. It was kind of a novelty to be eleven, twelve, thirteen, and fourteen years old and pull a business card out of my wallet while I told people that if they didn't get their paper, they could call my home. I only had to miss a few papers when delivering until I was totally cured of not being dependable or, in the case of my business card, reliable, because people would call the house and leave messages. My brothers would leave notes for me to call So-and-So, with reminders from all my brothers that I had forgotten to deliver the paper to a house, with a good laugh behind it.

I learned that if you put "reliable" on your business card, it's almost like an affirmation: if you don't become more reliable, you're going to have to change your business card to something else. I found it easier to follow through and deliver than to go back and pull all the cards I had handed out, and change that word to something else.

MY SHOE REPAIR BUSINESS

When you want to do something, you must assume the identity of someone who does that thing. For example, when I was a young boy and delivered newspapers, people would say, "Here comes the paper boy." For two hours every day, I stepped into the identity of being a paperboy.

When I was fourteen years old, I bought a shoe repair business. The grandfather of one of my grade school classmates was retiring and had his shoe repair business for sale. I asked my dad one day if he would go with me to look at a shoe repair business. He asked me many questions, like "How much does it cost?" and "Why do you want to fix shoes?" and "How are you going to get business?" and "Where are you going to put the machines?"

I told my dad, "He wants $900 for it, but I figure if we can meet with him a couple of times, the price will change. I don't know how much room the equipment will take."

I called the man, Jon Selenski, and asked if my dad and I could come and see his equipment. In a rich German accent, he replied, "Fine, I look forward to seeing you at 11:00 a.m. on Saturday."

Over the next six weeks, we met four times to measure the equipment, write down the model numbers, and count the inventory of repair materials, soles and heels. At the fourth meeting, I offered Mr. Selenski $650.00. I had made that money $0.017 (that's right, 1.7 cents per daily paper) at a time doing my paper route over the past three years.

Mr. Selenski agreed to my price and I pulled $650.00 from my wallet. I also asked him if he would write me a receipt, for I had learned a lot about paper work from my paper route as well. A few minutes later, we started loading some of the small stuff into our truck and then got ready for a big move. There were four big machines and eight other accessory tools. My two oldest brothers were very strong compared to me, then 120-pound, 14-year-old kid, and they helped my father and me move the equipment.

Landis stitching machine

I also applied to Milwaukee Area Technical College (MATC) to attend their shoe repair class. They allowed me to take the class as long as my father was willing to attend with me. I'm still very grateful that Dad always had time for me, as well as all of his other kids. Every Tuesday night for the next two years, my dad and I went to class. But I didn't wait to have my certificate to begin my shoe repair business. I was able to secure many customers from fire departments, police departments, churches, post offices, and some area businesses.

I used to tell the ministers and priests that while the work they do is saving souls, if they worked with me, I would

Finishing machine

Heel press

repair the whole thing. That little quip got many smiles from my clients and some business, too.

I scoured the neighborhood for shoes to repair, and from ages 14 to 19, through my business, I was able to make six to eight dollars per hour when the minimum wage was $1.10 per hour. It took about one year to make enough money to pay off my equipment and put my savings back in the bank. What had begun with less than two cents for a newspaper had grown into a nest egg that allowed me to move forward in my next venture.

Many times, I would get backed up ten to twenty pairs of shoes and quickly learned that it was easiest and most efficient to do about four to six pairs at one time. Sometimes, I would have all the shoes apart, which means taking off the soles and heels, and get too overwhelmed because I tried to do too many things at one time.

My shoe repair business really taught me firsthand the importance of the Chinese proverb, "Slow is fast." This means it is often most efficient and effective to slow down, develop a system, and follow it, rather than being in a hurry without a plan.

I learned how to introduce myself and my product. I encouraged people to bring their shoes needing repair to their workplaces in a grocery bag so that I could come by on my bicycle and pick them up. When the shoes were repaired, which took about two weeks, I would deliver the footwear and get paid. I learned about having proper inventory, not buying too much of one product, and making sure that the quality was high.

When my dad and I began the shoe repair business, he explained that it would be important to check the quality of one another's repairs before anything went out. On one occasion, a friend called me and said that his father had a pair of shoes to fix but wanted them back in a couple days. You might be familiar with the term "well-heeled," which means being prosperous. My friend's father apparently wanted to make a good impression.

It was a heel repair job. Having repaired heels about twenty times so far with my father, I decided I could do this emergency job by myself. So I took off the old heels, which had worn down. Following the process I had learned during shoe repair class, I inserted plugs in the holes where the old nails had been, glued on the new heels, waited for the glue to dry so that it would bond, and used the finisher to sand off the sides of the heel that always had to be trimmed to match the particular shoe.

However, I had forgotten to use a hole punch to push the nails in all the way. My friend's dad was at a Packer game the Sunday after I repaired the shoes and one of his heels came off. Well, I got a call that night asking if I guaranteed my work and the next day, I had a pair of shoes to repair a second time. After that, I always had my father inspect my work. I repaired my last pair of shoes when I was 19. I had somehow outgrown the business, but had learned life-long skills in the meantime.

GAS JOCKEY:
THE IMPORTANT TALK

When I finally turned sixteen, I started to work at a filling station as a gas jockey. In the early 1970s and before, you could drive into a gas station and the attendant would pump gas into your car, take the money, and bring back the change. He would wipe the windshield, check the oil and the air in the tires, and occasionally replace directional or taillights.

My boss was Tom Mulqueen, who also owned the gas station. He had four mechanics and six part-time gas jockeys. My older brothers had worked there before me, and I got to call him "Uncle Tommy." I also learned a lot of critical life lessons pumping gas, including "the important talk."

"The important talk" was given to me one Saturday morning when I arrived five minutes late to work. I did not punch in; I just started waiting on cars. I was supposed to be there at 8:00 a.m., so at about 10:30 a.m., when "the drive" (also known as the driveway) slowed down, Uncle Tommy called me into his office.

He motioned for me to sit down on one of the metal folding chairs across from his desk and asked, "Did you sleep last night?"

Immediately, I said, "Yes."

He pointed to his wall calendar and placed his grease-stained finger on yesterday's date. "Did you sleep this night?"

"Yes," I said quickly.

Then he pointed to the day before that and asked, "And this night?" Each time I answered yes. After going backward eight days, I answered with a bit of routine and impatience. That's when he hit me with "the lesson."

He said, "Did you eat any food yesterday? And the day before that?" He continued, going back four more days, and then he raised his voice to emphasize, "WHY?"

I said, "Because you have to sleep, and you have to eat."

"Would you agree that it is important?"

I said, "Sure."

Uncle Tommy leaned back in his creaky leather chair. "If some girl said to meet you tomorrow at 4:00 a.m. for a little kissy face, could you be there on time?"

"I could figure that out," I said, as I smiled.

Uncle Tommy grinned, "You bet! You could be there at 4:00 a.m.! And you would be there early and thinking about it all night long."

He leaned forward again and looked me straight in the eye. "Well, this job is your kissy face. So act like it is as important as eating and sleeping and fake it a bit better, okay?"

I was cured, converted and turned a new leaf in those few minutes. I was never late to that job again. From that moment forward, I always asked myself about whatever I was doing: "Is this important?"

Uncle Tommy's talk and insights have stayed with me for over four decades and I have thought of that experience literally thousands of times. I worked for "Uncle Tommy" until I was nineteen, doing all kinds of tasks. I was a bill collector, concrete apprentice, painter on some of his rentals, and errand boy.

It was a great opportunity, working with a guy like that. I learned many life lessons, as well as how to be an entrepreneur, from him. I am thankful for that opportunity and the lessons, which I still use today. Uncle Tommy was a great guy to work with and learn from. Incidentally, Uncle Tommy and Barney Karpfinger, one of my adopted dads, were very good friends in high school, the same private high school from which I graduated. Again, it's indeed a small world.

SEW WHAT?

As I got older, I was drawn to selling things. What did I sell? Anything, as long as I believed in it. I also knew that I had learned to fix shoes; I could learn to do embroidery as well.

Here's an other proverb for you to remember: "As more is created, more is consumed."

In 1984, I started my embroidery company with one embroidery machine and one account. I was 28. I had studied business and journalism at Marquette, but nothing prepared me for what I would learn over the next decade and a half.

Over the course of the next fifteen years, the company grew to have over eight hundred accounts, more than thirty machines, and sixty employees most of the time, with over one hundred employees during peak season. It was a crazy time for me; it was nerve-wracking and exciting at the same time. I had semi-trucks of clothing come in the door and go out the door in the matter of a day or two.

For six years, we embroidered NBA jerseys. Twenty-six thousand jerseys would come in the door and three days later, they would go out—all perfect, all accounted for, and on time.

*   *   *   *

When I had two embroidery machines, I remember thinking that when I have twelve machines, I'll be content. Perhaps you've heard of Maslow's Hierarchy of Needs: as more needs are satisfied, more needs are created. It was obvious that I was living with that philosophy. Psychologist Abraham Maslow, in 1943, listed these needs as the need for survival, safety, love, esteem, and self-actualization. In hindsight, I should have made my goal the attainment of a certain monthly income instead of a certain number of machines, because what I really wanted to do was create financial freedom, not own a lot of machines.

Properly defining your goals not only gets you closer to a desired outcome, it can also lighten the path along the way. What I really wanted to do was to make a lot of money so I could do a lot of different things, or maybe even do nothing. I remember hearing at a young age that money can't buy happiness, but it can buy freedom and freedom can make you happy.

I would occasionally observe my wealthy clients and notice that what they *had* wasn't that important, but what *had them*. How amazing to observe the confusing dynamics of what financial success and prosperity can bring.

* * * *

It wasn't until February, 1994, that I began to define with more clarity the things that I really wanted in my life. I was 38 years old, which turned out to be a mid-life crisis in some ways. I decided to train for the 1996 Olympic team. I was tired of working all the time and stressed out by trying to do too much. It appeared to be a logical escape because wrestling was something I was really good at and enjoyed.

The embroidery company; the author and Scott Grudzinski (1990).

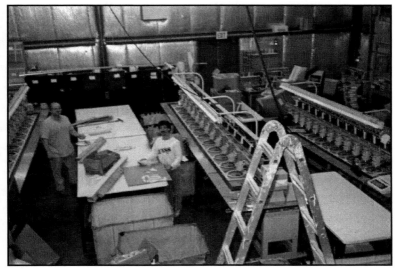

MORE ON RESISTANCE

Remember that I grew up in a blue-collar town called Cudahy, Wisconsin. There was a hardware store a few blocks from where I grew up that I wanted to buy in 1993 because I was hopeful I could make it a second location for my embroidery company. In 1996, the store became available and I bought the building. It needed a lot of work. The building was 10,000 square feet on two levels with a little apartment in the back.

The two-bedroom apartment had been built in the 1940s and provided the previous owner with living quarters for several years. My thought was to use it for several offices for the company. I must have given fifty people, many of them employees, a tour of the building and I'd often get to the back apartment. Because it was outdated and small, I'd say, "I can't imagine anyone living here," or "It's a nice little apartment, but I sure wouldn't want to live here."

As circumstances evolved, I sold my embroidery company and got it back a year later, because the purchasing group defaulted on the loan and it ended up being owned by a bank. A few months later, my cash locked up and the two-bedroom apartment I couldn't imagine anyone living in was the next place I lived.

I lived there for three years. When I moved in, I thought I was being disciplined by God or the Sovereign Hand or whatever you label as the Supreme Being. Three years went by and I learned a lot of lessons about being able to go back to your roots. It was an awakening about proper perspective.

The last few weeks I lived there, I was truly thankful to have a place to live. I was also able to let go of much of the sadness, regret, and the unforgiving thoughts I harbored about situations and people I previously labeled as having taken advantage of me. I shifted in my belief from thinking that things happened to me to deciding to make things happen using my intention and always being thankful for what I have experienced.

One day, about 10:00 on a Sunday morning, I lit a candle. I often meditate in front of a candle. I wrote down an affirmation that had been born out of a conversation a few days earlier with my friend Jos in Holland. I told him I really liked living in this apartment because I liked going to down to Lake Michigan as often as I wanted. The lakeshore was only about 15 minutes away, and I would often go down there to meditate, exercise and relax. I was in my late forties. I was truly thankful to have what I had. However, I wanted to have a place on a lake.

Seven hours later, my meditation was complete. My goal, as crazy as it might sound, was to experience the sentence, "I have the perfect place on the perfect lake." It took me several minutes to come up with that phrase because I initially had to have a certain price, a certain lake, that it had to be far from Milwaukee, and that I didn't have a big income at the time. All came up as limitations as I kept repeating the sentence; "I have the perfect place on the perfect lake."

Every time I would notice an obvious limitation, I stated the limitation and imagined it was being consumed by the candle flame I was looking at. As I did this hundreds of times, I noticed there were fewer and fewer obstacles or limitations in my experience. It was important for me to realize that I had to be in a "feeling" mode, not a "thinking" mode, so that I could intuitively notice what was coming up each time I would state my affirmation goal sentence.

Many of you who are reading this right now will make your own decision about this. Here's the challenge. Many people tend to judge things they don't understand. Remember, when you judge something, your attention is fixed and you are unable to see what's really there until you let go of your judgment.

Not resisting your judgment, I invite you to stay where you are and open the invitation to come someplace else. Maybe what I'm talking about really does work. My several-hour meditation could be explained as a day of prayer, if you want, but that is just another label.

There's a proverb that says, "Affirmation without action is lunacy." I was not naïve enough to think that I could sit with a candle all day and end up with the perfect place on the perfect lake without leaving the house.

On Monday morning, I called some friends who lived on lakes or knew people who lived on lakes. One of my friends had in-laws who live on Pine Lake, which is one of the most prestigious lakes in the area. His name is Frank. He said, "I don't know of anything right now and my in-laws have locked their house up for the winter, so that won't work. I'll put a note on my computer and ask the next ten people who come through, and maybe more than ten. As it comes up, I'll mention it."

The next day, a woman came into his office and saw the note: "Ask about lake home." She asked about it and he told her he knew someone who was looking to rent or housesit at a lake home. He had promised to ask some people this week to see if they might know someone who has a place available on a lake.

She said, "This is really crazy because last Thursday a really good friend of mine told me she and her husband are moving to California and want someone to housesit for them. They will probably be gone three to five years and then will probably come back to Wisconsin."

Frank gave her my number and on Wednesday afternoon, I was over on Pewaukee Lake looking at the place that I would be moving into three weeks later.

Remembering the words the artist from the State Fair told me when I was twelve years old: "It takes five minutes and thirty-two years," it was clear that my meditation took seven hours and three years of living in a place I resisted. My resistance created me living in the apartment and my acceptance of the situation opened the door for something better.

Then, having gone my course of house-sitting on Pewaukee Lake for five years, I knew I was nearing the end of my time at this place. I then lit another candle and created the primary intention of owning the perfect place on the perfect lake.

Three weeks later, I met a friend for dinner. She had worked in adoption law for many years and happened to be in my neck of the woods.

She said, "I can probably meet you at 7:00 p.m., but I have to stop at a property I own to get some stuff from the garage." I asked if I could help and she accepted. I met her at the house.

The house had two units, each consisting of two bedrooms, and looked out at a house that was on the lake. However, a few feet to the left of the house were 500 feet of lake frontage with access by a path to the lake. Four days later, I began painting and preparing my next place to live.

I don't share my way of doing anything as "the" way, but we keep doing the same things that work for us or often do the things that don't work for us if we have limiting beliefs. This continues until we develop an awareness that we want to change something.

No matter what beliefs you have about any aspect of your life, you will find that it is like a favorite color. Ask anyone his or her favorite color and regardless of the color, it will be that person's favorite one. Period. You will also find that favorite colors are not negotiable and neither are many of the beliefs people hold. By proper introspection and openness to improving aspects of your life, favorite colors might not change too easily, but your beliefs can.

THE MORE VERSATILE, THE MORE VALUABLE

The more versatile a person is, the more valuable he or she is to the team, the business, and to society in general. Whether in corporate America or the local food pantry, the person who is more versatile is always more valuable. When I coached a wrestler, I would never tell him he had a lot of talent. I would only tell him he had to focus on working harder so he could win by bigger margins, because no matter how good one is in this sport, there is always a buzz saw around the corner. There is someone coming up who can clean your clock, ruin your day, and show you why your head doesn't need to be as big as you thought it should be.

One of my outstanding high school teammates was Jerry Gates. He was plenty strong, but what was most impressive about Jerry was how he was excellent at everything. He had lots of friends, was at the top of my graduating class, and he won most of his matches. He was truly a big part of my success early on because he was the kind of guy who encouraged everyone to get better. As a team captain, he was an inspiration to all of us. He placed third in the state tournament two years in a row, 1973 and 1974, and was one of the last team members to score the points needed to put our team in the lead to win the team title.

After St. Thomas More High School, he went on to the University of Wisconsin–Madison and graduated with a degree in nuclear engineering.

When Jerry Gates and I graduated, St. Thomas More was an all-boys high school. It was an interesting group because the peer pressure was positive, focused on what you were going to do in the future.

I was not sure what field I wanted to go into, but did feel the pressure to get going and do something. I had already had a shoe repair business and wanted to learn something completely new to become more versatile and valuable in the workforce.

I applied to become a sheet metal journeyman in a union apprenticeship program. Because of their waiting list, it would be at least a year before I could be accepted into the program. In the meantime, I decided to enroll in the local community college, where the courses I took could eventually be transferred to a four-year college. I carried twelve credits per semester, attending classes at night, and working full time during the day for two semesters.

One of my first jobs was working for a plumbing contractor, making the pipes for the sprinkler business. After four months, I became the driver for the sheet metal division. My boss was a guy named Bob Krause. He was like an Army general. He always had an answer and really knew his stuff. He did all the scheduling for the company, making sure all the journeymen had the right equipment and supplies to do their work.

One day, I was delivering some sheet metal fittings to the downtown Milwaukee First Wisconsin Center, which was in the final stages of construction. As I was driving down the freeway, a piece of sheet metal flew off my truck and slid onto the road. I heard it clatter and saw it in my rear view mirror. As quickly as I could, I pulled over and got the piece of metal out of the right-hand lane. As I was putting it back on the truck, a deputy sheriff pulled up. He asked me what was going on. I told him what just happened and he informed me that there was a $75 fine for loss of load on an interstate.

I asked him with a puzzled look, "Now what?"

He asked me how long I had been driving truck. I told him it was my third day. He said, "Third day, for real?" and I said yes.

The sheriff said, "Well, I really shouldn't give you a ticket for something I didn't see, but I will give you a warning. I am going to call your boss and tell him you told me the truth about what happened and that you should be taught how to tie down the load."

At the shop, they made a new piece of sheet metal and I took it down to the construction site later that day.

The sheriff was true to his word and once again, I learned a valuable lesson. When I got back from my second trip downtown, my boss told me, "It looks like you had a big day today! I just want to tell you, you got off very easy with a phone call from a sheriff. When sheet metal flies off a truck, cars can get damaged, accidents can happen, people can be killed—a lot can go wrong!" I listened intently.

He continued, "I know you could have just driven on and we would have been short a piece for the job. I like that you hustled and I appreciate that you stopped to pick up the piece. So, in the future, let's hurry when hurry counts, like when you're loading or unloading the truck, and realize not everything can be hurried. Freddy, let me tell you to remember that 'slow is fast.'"

I was cured. My loads were tied down securely from then on.

The words of Bob Krause, one of my first bosses, have echoed in my ear tens of thousands of times over the last thirty-five years as I recalled that teaching moment.

"IT'S BETTER TO GET A LITTLE TOO LATE THAN TOO MUCH TOO SOON"

I remember seeing a *60 Minutes* show long time ago that featured Joe Paterno, the legendary football coach from Penn State University. The interviewer asked Coach Paterno if there was one sentence that would summarize all his coaching throughout the years, what would it be? He said, "It is better to get a little too late than too much too soon."

I have seen this myself firsthand over the years. In the sport of wrestling, some amazing talents don't make it in the program because they got too much, too soon. Athletes join programs and seem to catch on to wrestling very quickly. This can be very frustrating for the other athletes who don't have the same ability, even though it seems like a blessing to the gifted athletes. It can also be a curse to have something come too easily because sometimes the gifted athletes give up too soon when they have a hard time.

I can only say that it's a blessing sometimes that things do not come too easily. The next time you're working on a project and having difficulty, take a moment to reflect and see what is in the way of your success. You may notice that it is often just a bit of resistance on your part that's preventing you from reaching your goal. The fact is that what we resist really does persist. With that in mind, it is best to be clear in your goal, focused on your plan, and get going. There's no point in talking about the negative aspects of things unless it is to define a problem with the intention of solving it.

DEAR SON ...

I am often invited to speak at wrestling award banquets. The following letter was read by one of the fathers who happened to be a coach for the team. What impressed me about this father's was his great perspective on what it meant to be a coach and a parent. It doesn't always work out this way; sometimes parents put pressure on their kids and nobody wins.

Dear Son,

You had a tough time on the mat today and the ride home was pretty quiet. I admit I was very disappointed, but I later came to realize that I shouldn't be because it is all part of the journey you are taking.

When I watch you on the mat, I worry that you are doing battle while unprepared and that I have failed you in helping you prepare. As a father, that is my greatest fear - that you are unprepared to face the challenges that you will experience. I want you to be prepared for your match, but I've come to realize that it is the matches themselves that are, in the long run, win or lose, the things that ARE preparing you for wrestling and for life.

I think that the greatest benefit of wrestling is learning to face challenges and to demand the most of yourself. You learn to fight when you think there is no more fight left within you.

You learn to get up after you've fallen, time and time again. You learn about sacrifice and about pain. You learn to endure and to overcome. This is what I want for you, not because I wrestled, but because these lessons are the true gifts of this sport. Today's losses are actually part of this gift and an important part of your journey.

My dream for you is to not just win championships and fill your room with medals. My dream for you is much greater and I hope you get much more from wrestling. I hope you learn to strive for greatness even if you fail in the attempt. I hope you learn to get up one more time when you think you can't get up any longer. I hope you learn to not only face your fears, but to stare them down.

Wrestling isn't about winning. It is about the desire to win. It isn't about success, but rather the determination to succeed. I want you to succeed as a wrestler, not just to win state championships, but so you learn to be all that you can. This sport can help teach you that if you let it. I look forward to the seasons of our future as you go through these lessons and I'll be in your corner for each and every one of them.

I love you.
Dad

YOUR TEAM CAN BE BIGGER THAN ANY SPORT

J im Allen has helped hundreds of people in all kinds of ways, regardless of how they could help him. My success in reaching a leadership position at my insurance company began with Jim's helping hand.

In 2009, Jim Allen was inducted into the Marquette University Athletic Hall of Fame for his outstanding accomplishments as an athlete and a coach at Marquette and has been credited with bringing Marquette to national prominence during his tenure as cross country and track coach.

Fred McGaver, Jim Allen, and Dan Jones, 2009

THE 90-DAY TALK

In 1981, I was interviewing for jobs in sales with several companies. It was a real learning experience for me because I could ask questions, too, and often would. I had the opportunity to take about six jobs working in the construction industry and the brewing industry, but decided to take a commission-only position with a major insurance company.

I was interviewing with company A. One day, I was at Marquette University working out in the wrestling room after I graduated and remembered that the head track coach, Jim Allen, was an insurance agent.

I'd gotten to know Jim Allen very well over the years because his nephew, Tim Allen, was a high school classmate of mine, and his brother, Bob Allen, was a mentor to me over the years. I told Jim I'd been interviewing with an insurance company and was curious what he thought about it. He then asked me what my goals were. The next day, I met with his manager, who was named Herb, and who soon became my manager. Herb was twenty-five years older and had a law degree that he never used. He was the perfect guy for me to work for because he somehow pulled me out of the locker room, put a suit on me, and taught me many aspects of the insurance business that I still use today. As it worked out, Jim's office was right next to mine and the setting was perfect for me to learn about insurance.

For several weeks, I attended classes at the general agency to learn the very basics about life insurance. During this time, I was able to learn about many of the other companies and how they did business. I also learned about stepping into the identity of being an insurance agent. It was a big adjustment for me. Over the past several years, I have been a student, a cobbler, a wrestler, a coach, and now I was learning all over.

One day, I was reading a booklet published by the insurance industry about something called the "90-day Syndrome." The "90-day Syndrome" occurs when someone enters a new business and for the next 90 days, calls on all of his family and friends, hoping to peddle his product. You may experience this from time to time when friends join a multilevel marketing business and have a new product that you "just have to have." Part of my insurance agent training was developing a list of as many people I could think of from high school, college and, of course, family and friends.

My list included 386 people. I put the list in the envelope, signed the back, and wrote down June 1, 1982, one year after I contracted with my manager. He said, "You have to call on these people to get off to a fast start."

I responded, "I can get an appointment with most of these people, but as a friend, not as an insurance agent." I told him I learned in coaching that the difference between motivation and manipulation was always motive. I knew up front that my motive for meeting these people would not be pure, so I would not make a sale and at the same time, would strain my friendship with these people. I then told my manager that I would rather have a harder time getting an appointment with someone who only knows me in the context of insurance than to manipulate a friendship and then bring insurance into the conversation. From the handshake, i.e., from the beginning, I got off to a slow start.

I had three other people in my training class and all of them sold a policy within the first three weeks. I had been there three months and had not sold a policy. Nor was I able to request a draw of income because it was a commission-only position.

One day, after being in training for just over 90 days, Herb, my manager, called me into his office and said that we had to meet with his manager, Dennis, on Thursday at 2:00 p.m. and I agreed to do so. When the appointment rolled around, I found myself in a grand old mansion near Lake Michigan where over fifty insurance agents had their offices. My general agent's office was about 15 feet by 20 feet, it held a huge dark mahogany desk and had some cabinets on the wall that had been used in the previous century to store water for emergency fire situations.

I sat at the desk, my manager on my right, across from the general agent, who asked, "How are you doing, Fred?"

I began to tell him that I was learning more every day and was hopeful that I would soon be submitting some business.

He said, "Fred, are you sure you want to do this?"

I replied, "Yes, I am."

Herb, my district manager, mentioned a person who had been an agent for a while and decided that he wanted to be a banker, then another guy who wanted to work selling copy machines because that was a tangible product, a woman who wanted to work in a non-profit as an assistant. After about six or seven examples, I got that they were setting me up for the door, as in giving me my walking papers.

Upset, I got very quiet while my mind raced more than it had in a long time. I was focused on the conversation and at the same time trying to figure out how to handle the meeting to make sure that I didn't get sent down the pike, a.k.a. terminated. My general agent then said, "Fred, a lot of good people have left the insurance business and maybe that is where you need to be."

I stood up and walked over to the window, about fifteen feet away and said, "I got it. *(Long pause)* I got it. *(Longer pause)* I got this great idea." I then walked back across the room over to the tall cabinet and opened the door to find it was empty. I closed it, and then opened it, and I closed it, as I was saying, "This is a great idea. I am amazed. You are going to love this idea." I then walked back to the window with my arms stretched toward the ceiling and leaned against the window frame. I said it again. "This is really good."

After watching my performance, Herb asked, "Fred, what is the idea? Can you tell us?"

"Oh, yes. Here is my idea," I said as I walked back to my chair, but did not sit down.

I stood in the area where I would need to be if I were to take my seat again. Then I began. "Well, Herb, how long have you been selling insurance?"

He responded, "Fifteen years."

Then I asked Dennis how long he had been in the insurance business.

He said, "Thirty-five years."

"Great! Thirty-five years. Wow, I would love to read the book you could write."

I then walked over to the cabinet quickly as I was talking and then said, "Look at this. This is perfect. It will work out just great."

Dennis said, "Freddddddddddd" (with some annoyance in his voice).

As I walked back to the desk, I said, "Well, what we can do is put a mat in that cabinet."

"A mat?" Herb asked.

"Yes, a wrestling mat. I can get a mat from Marquette for a few months and we can store it there."

"Why do we need a mat?" asked Herb and I said, "So that we can work out together."

Dennis, looking completely blown away, said, "Wrestle!! Where? Here?"

"Yup. You'll wrestle and so will Herb."

After that, I slid off my wristwatch and as I was holding it in my hand, I reached across the desk so the watch was just under Dennis's chin.

I looked at Herb and said, "While Herb and I are wrestling, you can time us."

I then put the watch under Herb's chin, looked at Dennis and said "Then we will wrestle."

I held the watch under Dennis's chin again, looked at Herb and said, "We'll wrestle again while Dennis times us."

Then I held the watch under Herb's chin, but not so close this time, and said, "Then you will time us as we wrestle."

Then I moved the watch to Dennis's chin one more time, but this time he held his hands up to signal to me "not this again."

After taking my seat on the plush chair again, I leaned toward both men and said in a loud, confident voice, "This is what you can expect. You have been doing the insurance business for fifteen years and thirty-five years, respectively. I've been here for ninety-two days and you are going to whisper and send me out the back door. Well, if we can wrestle every Thursday for thirteen weeks and at the end of thirteen weeks, you guys aren't scoring on me, then you just quit. You just quit." I got even louder. "And if you bastards are not scoring on me, then I never want to see you do anything athletic—no Frisbees with the grandkids, no golf, no tennis. You just quit."

Then I got up, walked over to the window with my arms leaning against the window and said, "Yes, Fred, we are not going to call this a failure. In fact, no one really knows that you were here. You can just quit. Well, guys, I have a goal. In fact, I have few goals and two of them are to be in the business in five years from now and to make the Million Dollar Round Table next year. I am not going to quit today. I am going to get your workout gear ready and see you next Thursday at 2:00 p.m. I assume you wear an extra large, Dennis, and I figure you're a large, Herb." I then shook their hands, thanked them for all their help so far, and said I would see them soon. Ten steps later, I was out the door.

That was September 3, 1981, and about three weeks later, I sold my first policy for a grand commission of $108. Two weeks later, I sold another five policies for $2,120 and then week by week, I had more success.

Fast-forward to December 1982. I happened to be at a holiday open house at Jim Allen's home. It was Friday evening, December 22, the same week that all agency business had to be submitted for the final 1982 count. I got to the party about 6 p.m., even though it had started at 4:30. I was greeted by Jim's wife, Dolores. Within a few seconds, I had a drink in my hand and was greeted by other agents in the room.

As an aside, the wives of Dennis, Jim, and Herb—Mary, Delores, and Sharon, respectively, were always kind and encouraging, and I'll always be grateful for their friendship.

I started talking to my host, Jim Allen. As we were talking, Dennis, my general agent, walked over and greeted me. He called Herb from across the room. Now the four of us were standing in a circle and Herb congratulated me on a great year and making the Million Dollar Round Table.

Then Herb said, "Hey, Dennis how did we find this guy?"

He nudged Jim Allen and said, "It was you, Jim. You are how we got Fred."

Then Dennis said, "Yes, Jim, it was you. Thank you, Jim. Thank you." Dennis then said to Herb, "I remember how we could not get rid of him, too." Jim overheard the comment and laughed, "Dennis, what are you talking about?"

Herb then said, "We can tell. In fact, he'll appreciate this. Do you remember that day than we called you into the office downtown and we were going to make it easy for you to leave the business and you went off about the wrestling mat, wrestling with us, and even having an identity as an insurance agent and that you had to develop it and all you needed was time and you didn't need any money. You just needed time and that you were committed to working hard."

"Yes, I remember the whole thing," I said.

"Well, that day, Dennis and I sat there for about fifteen minutes, saying nothing to each other, wondering what had just happened. We were blown away and did not know what to do."

He continued. "Before you left, you said a couple of things that new agents have never told us before. You asked if you were costing us or NML any money. We agreed that you were not. Then you asked if it was a problem for anyone else that you had not written any business and Herb mentioned that people were wondering what was going on. I then asked them to have them call me and I would be glad to put them at ease. Then you dropped the bomb. You said you wanted to write some business and you would not get tired before we did. In the next week, you were going to keep working to figure it out. That was your goal and you were focused on getting your goal. We were both shocked and impressed at the same time. We were curious as to what would happen. You certainly had passion."

I think many of us quit too soon. We quit by making judgments, by making comments too soon without enough facts, and then we often just give up. We win a little each day or lose a little each day, so I think it is a pity to quit.

When I think of quitting, I am reminded of people who have committed suicide. Over the years, I've had some friends commit suicide. I wonder what could be the biggest punishment for suicide, if there were any punishment at all. Imagine this, you are at the gates with St. Peter and he says, "Hey, you came early. You are not scheduled to be here until fifty-five years from now," to the soul of a twenty-five-year-old man or woman. "Well, we are going to give you an option, since you came so soon. You get to see how your life would have turned out if you hadn't quit. So, get comfortable like you're in a movie. You will see that if you would've been a bit more open, honest, diligent, and levelheaded, it all would have worked out fine. You would have experienced love, prosperity, health, and friendship if you just hadn't quit."

Seeing that it would have worked would be punishment enough. Don't quit. Do a lot of things, but don't quit.

Since that "90 Day" talk, I have sold over $1,000,000,000 (yes, one billion) of life insurance.

DON'T HATE THE DETAILS; FALL IN LOVE WITH THEM

I once went to an insurance convention where the top twenty insurance salespeople in a company were being honored. The presenters paraded the honorees across the stage and talked briefly about each person, showing a picture of the honoree and the honoree's family and staff. The presenter would also ask each person what he or she most liked about the business and what the honoree considered the biggest obstacle.

One year, back in the mid-1980s, seven of the top twenty said, "I hate details."

I thought, "What a pity, because we hear that the devil is in the details."

We all know that the smallest detail can be the most important thing in our lives. Ask anyone who has had a blocked vein or a blood clot or an aneurysm. The smallest details.

From practicing my sport, as well as my many business ventures, I have learned to fall in love with the smallest detail. When you master details back to back, you are creating a path of excellence. That path will take you to new levels of mastering whatever you embrace and new levels of understanding yourself more deeply.

When young athletes embrace the process of drilling a move repeatedly, thousands of times, with focus on the process, they will be able to master that move. What is the purpose of our lives, if not living to master all kinds of things? Mastering a move or a sport is just a metaphor for other things at which we may want to excel.

WORK AT PLAY
AND PLAY AT WORK

As I look back, there was definitely a time when I was unable to relax completely. I was so immersed in my workaholic tendencies that I just had to go all out or I didn't feel that what I was doing would make a big enough difference for me to meet whatever goal(s) I was focused on.

One thing Coach Knitter taught me in high school was the importance of a schedule. Before the season even started, he had our whole season mapped out, with starting times and ending times. He provided the schedule to all his athletes and their parents so they could plan other family activities. Sometimes after big meets, he would schedule an hour workout instead of a two-hour workout and twice a season, he would give us a day off in lieu of a scheduled workout. He instilled in us to really work hard while we were working out, because we could be sure the other schools were practicing hard and we didn't want to fall behind. Coach Knitter's constructive peer pressure was a great tool that helped us all improve and keep our focus.

In the insurance business and professionally, I see many people who take their vacation fifteen minutes at a time, meaning they never come to work to really work and when they go home, they can't play because they didn't work at work. It's not important whether they're stuck or overwhelmed, because on some level, they're just not going to relax and they're not going to do it, whatever "it" is. This leads me to wanting things too badly.

Simply said, if you're going to play at work, leave work and go play. If you have to work at play, you're probably working too hard, or not hard enough, or are in the wrong career.

LOOKING INTO OTHER PEOPLES' POCKETS

I once had a conversation with an insurance agent mentor. He was telling me about working with successful businessmen as they implemented insurance programs. One thing he told me was to not keep score of what they make as a way to diminish yourself and not to look into someone else's pocket who has less than you and think, "That poor sap."

You will find the people who have lots of money often don't have the time to look into someone else's pocket because they're too busy counting their own. Be the guy who counts his own and you won't be distracted with having more or less than anyone else. Best said is the prayer, "Lord, Don't let me have too little that I despise you or that I have too much that I forget you."

SARCASM

A sharp, bitter or cutting remark; jibe or taunt.

J ust after I graduated from high school in 1974, I met a guy who did handwriting analysis. When he analyzed my handwriting, I was completely amazed at how revealing my handwriting was and how he could identify so many of my personality traits with ease and accuracy. I was so impressed with the science of graphology, or handwriting analysis, that I began to learn about it myself. A bookcase full of books on handwriting, many seminars on handwriting analysis later, and having analyzed in the tens of thousands of various handwriting samples, I'm extremely confident that what I learned is very accurate and revealing about anyone who uses cursive handwriting.

One trait that commonly shows up in handwriting is sarcasm. People often justify a snappy answer or teasing comment as being quick-witted. I used to joke around a lot, too, until one day a mentor told me how destructive sarcasm was. If you knew how destructive sarcasm is in your life, you'd stop doing it right now.

I remember saying to him, "You can't change things quickly if you've been doing them a long time."

He said, "You're right, especially when you say you can't change things quickly. When you say that you can change things and not put a limitation or expectation on how quickly the change takes place, then it can be pretty effortless."

He gave me a little exercise to do. He told me to carry a pad of paper and writing instrument at all times. "When you're in a situation that you notice that you want to make a sarcastic remark, refrain from saying anything. Pull out your pad and pen and write down the incident. For example, the incident may have involved someone doing something you considered stupid. Number your answers from 1 to 10 as you describe the event, and write down your ten responses.

He continued, "You might not be able to do this every time. You'll notice that people you're sarcastic with are the ones you are closest to. You're unlikely to be bold and sarcastic with people you don't know well because you don't want to be misunderstood."

Sarcasm causes misunderstanding. Some people say, "I was just kidding." That's not really true. When people are sarcastic, there is a tinge of anger in their voices, even though their words might come across with a smile. There is also an aspect of a condescending attitude toward the other person.

I've found that when I want to say something sarcastic and I've taken time to write down my reaction ten times, my words become much more gentle and loving by the time I've completed the exercise. I create ten different answers to the comment or situation. By the time I get to answer number seven, eight, nine or ten, the answers are very kind, loving, and more in line with what I wanted to communicate all along.

Sarcasm destroys relationships, limits communication, and hinders the ability for your best intentions to be shared or received. You can be sarcastic, but not without a price. The price is miscommunication, which often leads to regret, guilt, or damage control.

FREDDY MCGAVER'S
LIFE LESSONS

&

THE LIFE-CHANGING
POWER OF MENTORING

MENTORING

All the concepts presented in this book represent aspects of the power of mentoring. Mentoring happens every day in big and small ways. It can be as simple as asking a question of someone who seems to need guidance or as complex as a formal mentoring program in a business, religious or educational institution. Mentoring relationships may be short term or long term—it just depends on the people involved and their needs. The only requirement of a mentoring relationship is that the parties involved intend to help one another grow and develop.

Personal growth and development requires commitment on the part of the individual, as well as the support of mentors. Mentoring is different than teaching or coaching because mentoring shapes the outlook and attitudes of the mentee. Teachers teach information, such as history and biology. Coaches teach skills, such as the wrestling moves that helped me throughout my athletic career. Mentors, however, taught me the attitudes and outlook required to excel at wrestling. I could have had great skills, but would not have succeeded without the proper perspective. Many times, mentors are also coaches and teachers.

The great thing about strong mentor-mentee relationships is that both parties learn from one another. I've often heard mentors say they learn more from those they are mentoring than they feel the mentee might learn from the mentor. In order for this to happen, ego needs to be put aside and each person open to learning and experiencing new ideas.

Mentoring can occur in many ways, both formal and informal. Formal mentoring relationships are developed as part of institutional business mentoring programs, at schools, and so on. Informal mentoring relationships often develop between people of different ages or with different skill sets. My coaches, for example, coached in ways that helped me improve as a wrestler, but also mentored me as I changed how I looked at things in general because of their influence. The respect, work ethic, competitiveness, honesty, creativity and other ideas introduced to me through mentorship in wrestling have helped me succeed in life. They have also helped me to recover from difficult times because I have the confidence to know I have the skills needed to succeed at the things I choose to do. Informal mentoring, as I experienced through Mrs. Barrer, one of my neighbors growing up, had an equally large effect on my development as a person.

Mentoring relationships can be challenging, especially at first. In many cases, a mentor will go down the mentee's path with him and learn as the mentee learns. In other instances, the mentor will notice a behavior or attitude that is unproductive for the person expressing it. In these cases, the mentee is often unaware of the problem and may not be open to suggestions for change. In this situation, the mentor will often try to figure out ways to gently suggest or model appropriate behaviors or attitudes. This type of communication is often very subtle, so it is likely to take time for the mentee to understand, accept and adapt new behaviors and attitudes.

There are situations in which the mentee must learn a lesson in a rapid and complete way. In these cases, the mentor will push the mentee to change, think differently, change her self-determined identity (i.e. slacker, loner) to something more positive, and realign his or her values so they best serve his/her life.

Finally, a successful mentoring experience will include a frank discussion of what was learned, how useful the knowledge is to the mentee (and/or mentor), and perhaps even discussion of how the mentee will apply the knowledge learned to future activities.

One of the key techniques mentors of all types use is taking advantage of teachable moments. For example, if you observe someone engaging in a disruptive behavior and your mentee is with you, it could lead to a discussion of why the behavior is inappropriate and what could be done to improve or avoid the situation in the future.

Anyone can be a mentor. We all have something to offer. All we have to do is be aware of the mentoring opportunities presented to us and take the opportunity to learn. As my co-author Sue asks when facing a challenge, "What is the lesson I'm supposed to learn?" Each challenge is an opportunity to give or receive mentorship. When you reach out to others—either as mentor or seeking mentoring, you can't help but grow.

MUSINGS FROM THE MAT

Thank you for letting me share some of my stories with you. There are many more, enough to make this book ten times longer. If you think about it, each of our lives is a work in process, and much like the premise of Maslow's Hierarchy of Needs, in which he states that as one of our human needs is satisfied, more needs are created. To me this means that the more introspective we become about our life paths, we continue to discover more areas we can explore more deeply.

I've decided that going deeper is important to me because that's how I continue learning powerful lessons. Going deeper also helps me understand the bigger picture of why I'm here. Experiences I once viewed as failures, when put into perspective, were merely some events that happened before my next breakthrough.

One of my father's favorite sayings was, "If you work hard and do a good job, you will be rewarded."

"It all works out," were Larry O'Neil's favorite words of wisdom.

"Stay focused and do the next thing," are words of Barney Karpfinger's I'll never forget.

"It's OK to try new things, but be willing to work hard to increase your chances of success," I recall my father saying.

The words of my three dads have continued to guide me throughout my life, and probably will go on until I am no more. They could be viewed as casual comments or as fundamental foundations for building a better life.

For many years, I told people I worked with on different business projects that, "There is no hurry on this one. Let's just do it now." Sometimes they would be annoyed with my intense focus because what I happened to be working on would not necessarily be their top priority.

We may have unlimited personal preferences, but we all have a common need and desire to make a difference in the lives of others. Such an attitude improves our own lives, as well.

I invite you to embrace a challenge. If you truly want to improve your life, you can make a decision right now, in this instant, by declaring that this moment is a turning point from whatever your life was or is, to what it could be as you make a positive impact on the lives of others. However, before you make this potentially impulsive decision, I need to share with you a couple of other insights.

There is a proverb that states, "Nice and easy does it every time." It speaks to the concept of relationships where, typically, a man and a woman become friends, then better friends, and then one day, they discover they have a lot in common, and decide to pursue a life together. I personally believe that "nice and easy" does it every time. An impulsive "yes" can lead to an impulsive "no."

Albert Einstein was quoted as saying, "Insanity is doing the same thing over and over again and expecting different results." For many people, getting the same results is the perfect place to be. There's nothing wrong with that; it's just the path they have chosen for themselves.

We all get what we give. The more positive the giving, the more positive the getting is as well. As we reach out to others, learn about their needs and wants, and share the positive aspects of their passions and interests, we will discover the many commonalities. I repeat: we all want to make a difference in someone else's life. We are each on our own path and have the power to decide whether or not we stay in a routine or embrace the opportunity to grow and develop. One way to open yourself to growth is to appreciate and acknowledge the positive things and events you see around you every day. Every day, look for an opportunity to do three important things:

- Applaud the good works being done by others,
- Inform people about the positive aspects of your community, and
- Invite them to participate on a deeper level.

It's OK to be stuck, and most of us have been stuck in one way or another. However, being stuck is an excuse for avoiding getting unstuck and moving on to a deeper, happier, more fulfilling life. I promise that the moment you decide to start making a positive difference by becoming an "ambassador of encouragement." that you too will experience great benefit.

We all get what we give! Let's give good stuff!

TO CONTACT THE AUTHOR

Please contact the author at
www.theMagicofMentorship.com
to order books or to schedule Freddy McGaver
as a speaker for your organization.